# HOW IMMIGRANTS FARE IN U.S. EDUCATION

**Georges Vernez ◆ Allan Abrahamse**

**with Denise Quigley**

*Institute on Education and Training*
*ter for Research on Immigration Policy*

Supported by
The Andrew W. Mellon Foundation

RAND

## PREFACE

Continuing increases in the number of immigrant children and youths in American schools and colleges raise the dual questions of how they affect these educational institutions and how they perform in them. These youths will eventually enter a national economy that is in transition and that will demand more educated workers and fewer less-educated workers. This report examines the participation and performance of immigrant children in U.S. primary, secondary, and higher education. It also identifies the individual and family factors that are associated with immigrants' and natives' educational attainment.

This report is one of three RAND reports that examine the participation of immigrants in the nation's educational system. The other two reports focus on the effects of increasing immigration on U.S. schools and on higher education institutions, respectively:

Lorraine M. McDonnell and Paul T. Hill, *Newcomers in American Schools: Meeting the Educational Needs of Immigrant Youth*, Santa Monica, Calif.: RAND, MR-103-AWM/PRIP, 1993.

Maryann Jacobi Gray, Elizabeth S. Rolph, and Elan Melamid, *Immigration and Higher Education: Institutional Responses to Changing Demographics*, Santa Monica, Calif.: RAND, MR-751-AMF, 1996.

The project was sponsored by the Andrew W. Mellon Foundation and the RAND Institute on Education and Training with funds from the Lilly Endowment.

This report and its companions should interest anyone involved in the interactions between immigration and the U.S. educational system including federal, state, and local policymakers and administrators; advocates; school and college administrators and teachers; and researchers.

# CONTENTS

# FIGURES

# TABLES

A growing number of immigrant children and youths have entered the country over the past 25 years. In 1990, there were more than 2.3 million immigrant children and youths in U.S. schools and colleges—about 5 percent of all students.

Many of these children have to overcome poor academic preparation in their country of origin and nearly all have to learn English and new institutional and cultural customs and norms. As a result, there are growing concerns about how these children are performing in U.S. schools and postsecondary institutions and in turn about the new set of demands they are placing upon these institutions. These concerns are exacerbated by the increasing diversity of languages and cultures that these students bring with them and their high concentration in a few areas of the country. About 75 percent of these children are concentrated in California, Florida, Illinois, New York, and Texas. California's educational institutions alone are currently educating more than two out of five of the country's immigrant children and youths.

This study is the first effort to systematically describe and analyze the experience and performance of immigrant children and youths in the U.S. educational system. Two companion studies have explored the new demands these children and youths are placing on U.S. primary and secondary schools and on colleges, respectively, and how those institutions are responding to these demands.[1]

---

[1]McDonnell and Hill (1993) and Gray and Rolph (1996).

## METHODS AND LIMITATIONS

We used data from "High School and Beyond" (HSB), a national representative sample of more than 21,000 10th and 12th graders first interviewed in 1980 and followed over a six-year period through their high school years, graduation, and postsecondary education in U.S. colleges. These data were complemented with data from the 1970, 1980, and 1990 U.S. Census of Population and Housing to analyze participation in U.S. education across all age groups and over time.

Throughout this study we compare the participation and performance of immigrant children and youths in U.S. educational institutions to that of their native counterparts overall and within each of the four major racial/ethnic groups: Asian, black, Hispanic, and white.

The HSB data have two major limitations. First, they provide information on immigrant students and natives who began their education before 1980. The number of immigrant children in the nation's schools has doubled since then, and schools' and colleges' ability to absorb them has arguably deteriorated. Hence, today's immigrants may perform differently from those of 15 years or so ago. Second, HSB findings are restricted to immigrants who were in a U.S. school by the 10th grade. Immigrant youths who entered the U.S. education system after that grade are not included.

## EXPERIENCE IN PRIMARY AND SECONDARY EDUCATION

Immigrant children and youths are as likely as natives to enroll in U.S. primary and middle schools. However, they are somewhat less likely than natives to attend high school: In 1990, participation rates were 87 and 93 percent, respectively. All of this differential is accounted for by immigrant youths of Hispanic origin, primarily from Mexico. In 1990, one of every four immigrants from Mexico in the 15–17 age group was not in school—a rate nearly 20 percent lower than that for any other immigrant group and 17 percent lower than that for natives of Mexican origin.

We present evidence suggesting that the relatively low in-school participation rates of Mexican immigrants of high school age is primarily due to their not "dropping in" to the school system in the first place rather than their "dropping out" of school.  By age 15, Mexican immigrants have already been out of school in Mexico for two years on average.  They do not enroll in U.S. schools either by choice, because of inability to catch up with others their age or their native counterparts, or by economic necessity because they must support themselves and their families.

Conditional on having been enrolled in a U.S. high school by grade 10, immigrant students are more likely than their native counterparts to make choices consistent with eventually pursuing a college education.  They are more likely to follow an academic track and take advanced courses in math and sciences.  These differences in course-taking patterns hold not only in the aggregate but also within each racial/ethnic group.  However, there are variations among immigrants of different racial/ethnic groups just as there are such variations among natives.  Asian immigrants generally performed best on indicators of preparation for college, followed by white and black immigrants.  Hispanic immigrants performed the lowest on nearly all indicators of college preparation.

Immigrants in U.S. high schools are also more likely to plan to go to college and to report working hard to achieve their expectations.  Similarly, the immigrant parents of immigrant children report higher educational expectations for their children than native parents do.

Immigrant children and parents of all racial/ethnic groups studied have higher educational aspirations than their native counterparts.  However, this difference in aspirations is three times greater between immigrants and natives of Hispanic origin than it is between immigrants and natives in other groups.  This significant decline in the educational aspirations of Hispanics in the United States has also recently been noted by other researchers.  Its causes, however, have yet to be thoroughly investigated.

## HIGH SCHOOL GRADUATION AND COLLEGE-GOING

Whatever difficulties immigrant children and youths might face adjusting to the language and institutional and cultural norms of this country, their educational attainment has equaled if not exceeded that of native children and youths.  Immigrant high school sophomores were just as likely as natives to graduate from high school within four years from their sophomore year—with Asians more likely to graduate than whites, blacks, and Hispanics, in that order.

Immigrant high school graduates were also more likely than their native counterparts to enroll in postsecondary education, attend college, and stay continuously through four years of college. Immigrants' higher rates of participation in higher education hold within each racial/ethnic group. But there are differences between immigrants of different racial/ethnic groups that mirror the well known differences between natives of different racial/ethnic backgrounds. Asian immigrants and natives scored generally the highest on all indicators of college-going and Hispanic immigrants and natives scored consistently the lowest on indicators of college-going with whites and blacks in between. The differences are large. Four of every five Asian high school graduates go on to college, compared to one of every two Hispanic high school graduates.

In multivariate analyses, we found that the individual and family factors associated with college-going were generally the same for immigrants and natives as well as across racial/ethnic groups. High school graduates whose parents have higher income, higher levels of education, and higher educational expectations for their children are more likely to pursue a college education than others. This confirms the importance of family background and family attitudes toward education in determining children's eventual educational attainment. Also, a student's positive attitude toward working hard in school was found to be positively associated with college-going for all groups. All else equal, immigration status per se was not found to be associated with college-going.

The fact that Hispanics have lower scores than Asians, whites, and blacks on nearly all key family and individual characteristics— income, parental education, and educational aspirations—helps explain their lower educational attainment.

## POLICY IMPLICATIONS

Our findings suggest that there is no need to develop policies targeted *uniquely* on immigrants. This does not mean, however, that the increasing number of immigrants in U.S. schools does not place new and unique demands upon the educational institutions serving them.  Two companion studies (McDonnell and Hill, 1993; Gray and Rolph, 1996) have documented the difficulties that schools and colleges are having meeting the special language and social support needs of immigrants and the resource strains they place on schools' overall operations.  The growing presence of immigrants in U.S. educational institutions also raises fundamental questions regarding graduation requirements, most particularly with regard to English proficiency, equity in the allocation of financial aid, and the definition of "disadvantaged" and "underrepresented" students in the face of increased diversity.  Until now, these questions have been either ignored or addressed  ad hoc, leading to inconsistencies within and across institutions.  They should now be addressed.

Beyond that, the continuing large discrepancy in educational attainment between Hispanics and other racial/ethnic groups should be cause for concern.  After 25 years of continuous and growing immigration, Hispanics are rapidly becoming the largest minority in the United States.  Already one out of three high school students in California is of Hispanic origin and this proportion will continue to grow in years to come regardless of whether or not there is continuing immigration.  It is not going too far to suggest that the educational attainment Hispanics eventually reach will in large measure determine the quality of the future labor force and the demand for public services in key states of the country.

Enhancing the educational achievements of Hispanics  and other similarly situated students—will require policies that go beyond the classroom.  Income assistance and financial assistance can alleviate the income gap between Hispanics and those of other groups.  But public funding for these programs is being reduced and at the same time college tuition and fees are going up rapidly.  Also, low levels of parental education and low educational expectation of parents and students may not be easily amenable to change.  Programs directed at increasing parental involvement in the education of their children and adult education programs including English language instruction, high school equivalency classes, vocational education, and workshops on effective parenting are steps in the right direction.  But demand for these programs far exceeds supply.

We also need to understand why the educational expectations of parents and students are declining across generations of immigrants, xvi How Immigrants Fare in U.S. Education

most particularly Hispanics. This understanding is necessary if strategies are to be developed to effectively address this problem.

Finally, strategies need to be developed to encourage Hispanic immigrant youths age 14 to 17 to pursue their education in this country. Failure to do so will result in hundreds of thousands of youths without a high school diploma with no prospects for economic mobility over their lifetime.

# ACKNOWLEDGMENTS

We thank our colleagues Maryann Jacobi Gray, Kevin McCarthy, Elizabeth Rolph, and Bob Schoeni for help in conceptualizing the issues and for guidance throughout this effort. We also thank the members of the RAND Center for Research on Immigration Policy Advisory Board for their insightful comments in the course of this effort. Throughout this project, Stephanie Bell-Rose, program officer at the Andrew W. Mellon Foundation, provided intellectual and financial support and a forum for sustained discussions among a variety of researchers and practitioners on different aspects of immigration policy and the immigrant experience.

This report benefited from the thorough reviews of Rebecca Kilburn (RAND) and Raul Hinojosa (UCLA). Their suggestions for presenting and interpreting the materials were most useful. But they are not responsible for the report's shortcomings.

Karla McAffee's efforts in preparing the report are much appreciated.

# Chapter One

# INTRODUCTION

The United States is closing the 20th century the way it began: with a substantial level of immigration that is hastening population growth and reshaping the U.S. ethnic composition. The number of foreign-born people residing in the country has more than quadrupled since Congress liberalized immigration policy in 1965, reaching 22 million in 1994. By 1994, 8.5 percent of the U.S. population was foreign-born, up from 5 percent in 1965.[1] Currently, nearly one million additional persons immigrate every year, accounting for more than 40 percent of the nation's yearly population growth. Whereas yesterday's immigrants came predominantly from Europe, today's immigrants come from all parts of the world, with Asians and Hispanics accounting for more than 80 percent.

Earlier waves of immigrants tended to concentrate on the East Coast, most particularly in New York. Today's immigrants tend to concentrate on the West Coast, most particularly in California, where nearly two out of every five new immigrants settle. The large metropolitan areas of Florida, Illinois, and Texas also harbor a large concentration of new immigrants. Like their predecessors, today's immigrants are predominantly young, with a majority having received little schooling in their native countries, and many having suffered the traumas of economic deprivation, war, or both.

Although most immigrants enter the country as adults, a sizable proportion enter when they are still of school age. In 1990, more than

---

[1]Although the current number of immigrants is the highest at any time in U.S. history, its proportion in the U.S. population is lower than in any decade from the middle of the 19th century until the 1930s, when it ranged from 13.2 to 14.7 percent.

two million immigrants, 11 percent of the total foreign-born population, were age 17 or below.  Many of these children enter U.S. schools and some have to overcome poor academic preparation in their own country.  And nearly all of them have to learn English and new institutional and cultural customs and norms.  Numerous anecdotal accounts tell of the difficulties these children and youths encounter adjusting to and finding their place in U.S. schools and postsecondary institutions.  In turn, concerns have been raised that immigrants in U.S. schools and colleges, with their perceived unique needs, are not given the attention they may require, thereby affecting their educational opportunities as well as their opportunities for eventual success in the U.S. labor market.  Since immigrants constitute more than one-fourth of the growth of the national labor force, their preparation for work is of importance for the future of the U.S. economy.  At the same time, those who are closest to immigrants in school—the teachers, professors, and administrators in our educational institutions—often describe these youths as highly motivated and eager to integrate successfully into school as well as into the broader American society.

This study is the first comprehensive effort to describe and analyze the experience of immigrant children and youths from all parts of the world in the U.S. education system.  It examines the extent to which immigrants of school age actually enroll in U.S. schools and how they fare in this system from middle school, to high school, and eventually to college.  This first chapter outlines the research questions and briefly reviews what is known about the performance of immigrants in U.S. schools and the factors that affect it.  The chapter then outlines the data and methods used in this study.

## RESEARCH QUESTIONS

This study focuses on three questions:

- To what extent do immigrant children participate in U.S. primary and secondary education?

- How well do U.S. high schools prepare immigrant students for college and what are these students' college-going rates?

- What individual and family factors affect immigrants' educational attainment?

These questions are addressed for immigrants as a whole and for each major racial/ethnic group, and their educational attainment is compared to that of native-born students as a whole and also by racial/ethnic groupings.

## PAST RESEARCH

Research on the educational and economic mobility of immigrants has focused primarily on immigrant adults, to the relative neglect of immigrant children.[2] With a few notable exceptions (Caplan et al., 1989; McDonnell and Hill, 1993; Carnoy, Daley, and Hinojosa, 1993; and Kao and Tienda, 1995), most of the research on the educational experience and performance of immigrant children is ethnographic. It has focused on the experience of immigrant children in primary and secondary schools, not those in college, and on specific and different immigrant groups. In brief, these studies are rich in textured descriptions in specific school settings but do not permit generalizations to all immigrant youths either within a state or nationally.

Three major findings emerge from these studies.[3] First, immigrant children and youths face a broad array of "special" educational needs and problems. Learning English is but one of those needs. Problems include high residential mobility; coping with emotional stresses due to adjustments to new social norms and a new institutional environment, and/or traumas due to war, family disruptions, or separations; poverty; and inadequate social support to compensate for broken community ties in their native countries and loss of support necessary for psychological well-being (McDonnell and Hill,

---

[2]A rich literature has examined the economic mobility of immigrant adults. For a review of this literature, see Greenwood and McDowell (1990) and Borjas (1994). For a more recent review, see Schoeni, McCarthy, and Vernez (1996). This latter study compares the experience in the U.S. labor market of immigrants from various countries of origin.

[3]This subsection relies on a review of past research contained in McDonnell and Hill (1993), pp. 5–10. It is updated with the findings of more-recent studies and complemented with a review of the literature specific to the college experience of immigrants.

1993; Suárez-Orozco and Suárez-Orozco, 1993; Caplan et al., 1989; and Duran and Weffer, 1992). Studies of Latino and Chinese immigrants' acculturation at the college level suggest that these students suffer higher levels of stress than nonimmigrants and those immigrating at an earlier age (e.g., Meana, Padilla, and Maldonado, 1987; Padilla, Alvarez, and Lindholm, 1986; and Sue and Zane, 1985). Evidence of acculturation stresses was also identified for students from Africa (Pruitt, 1978). Specific sources of stress at the college level include the role of family, values, social behaviors, and student expectations (Fernandez, 1988).

Whether such stresses influence educational achievement in U.S. schools and colleges has not been thoroughly investigated. Some studies suggest that immigrants may still achieve at high levels but have to compensate for language difficulties by limiting their choice of major, studying longer hours, and taking fewer courses than other students (Sue and Zane, 1985; Fernandez-Barillas and Morrison, 1984; Graham, 1983; and Searle and Ward, 1990).

Second, there is mounting recent evidence that immigrant youth do comparatively well in primary and secondary schools. McDonnell and Hill (1993) reviewed the transcripts of 745 students enrolled in two elementary, two middle, and two high schools in Los Angeles. They concluded that by their senior year in high school, immigrants—25 percent of whom had entered U.S. schools at the high school level—were just as likely, if not more likely, to take college "gatekeeper" courses than their native counterparts. These college preparatory courses include algebra, geometry, laboratory sciences, history, and regular or advanced English courses, which are required for admission to many four-year colleges. Using data from a national sample of 8th graders followed through 12th grade, Kao and Tienda (1995) conclude that children of immigrants—both born abroad or in the United States—earned higher grades and math and reading scores than other students after controlling for socioeconomic characteristics. These studies are consistent with earlier ethnographic studies suggesting that:

> in many cases, they [immigrants] do better academically and persist in school longer than native-born majority-group peers of similar class backgrounds, or even frequently, of the middle class (Gibson, 1988, p. 173).

The studies suggest several factors that may contribute to this pattern. One factor is that immigrant students are more motivated, have higher aspirations, and are willing to work harder than other students (Gibson, 1988, 1993; Duran and Weffer, 1992; Caplan, Whitmore, and Choy, 1989; and Rumbaut, 1990). Another factor is self-selection: Immigrants are predisposed to adapt to the host society and eager to do what is necessary to achieve economic mobility (Chiswick, 1979; Borjas, 1990; and Ogbu, 1991). High parental expectations that place a high normative value on education—as well as behavioral reinforcement that sets aside time and space for homework—is yet a third factor that has been suggested to explain the relative success in school of immigrant children (Kao and Tienda, 1995; Caplan, Whitmore, and Choy, 1989; and Rumbaut, 1990). Finally, some note that teachers prefer teaching immigrants because they are "more motivated and bright" than are native-born students (McDonnell and Hill, 1993) and hence, may institutionally favor immigrants (Gibson, 1993). Which of these factors, and possibly other factors, are most important in explaining the educational achievement of immigrant children remains to be identified.

No study has yet focused on the immigrant youths' participation and attainment in postsecondary education. However, Kao and Tienda (1995) have found that children of immigrants have higher college aspirations than the native-born children of native-born parents.

Third, the few studies that compare immigrant groups from different regions/countries of origin find significant differences among them. A major distinction made has been between Asians and other groups of immigrants. However, Kao and Tienda (1995) found that:

> Net of immigrant status, student and parental characteristics, Asians earned grades similar to their white counterparts. This finding qualifies prior comparisons indicating that Asians outperform whites. Consistent with other studies, black and Hispanic youth earned grades below those achieved by whites. However, and possibly because of difficulties with English, all minority groups achieved lower reading scores than their white counterparts. Black and Hispanic youth also earned lower math test scores. Despite the lower performance of minorities relative to whites, their educational aspirations are equivalent to or higher than whites from comparable family backgrounds (p. 9).

Factors that may explain this pattern across racial/ethnic groups range from differential academic preparation and aspirations developed in the country of origin, differences in family environment, and cultural differences due to a group's own culture and its initial terms of incorporation into American society (Ogbu, 1991).

In brief, past studies suggest that although immigrants have a number of difficulties to overcome in U.S. educational institutions, they are generally successful in doing so. They also suggest that there may be significant differences among immigrant groups. However, these studies are often idiosyncratic with respect to communities or schools, immigrant groups, and/or level of schooling considered. Hence, their findings cannot be generalized either to immigrants nationwide, or across immigrants within a racial/ethnic group and across various levels of schooling.

## METHODS

### Data

This study relies primarily on data collected from a 1980s' national longitudinal survey of high school sophomores and seniors known as "High School and Beyond."[4] To look at trends over several decades, we complement these data with data from the 1970, 1980, and 1990 U.S. Census of Population and Housing.

"High School and Beyond" (HSB) contains data from a national sample of 10th and 12th graders first interviewed in 1980.[5] All of these high school sophomores and seniors were followed at two-year intervals over a six-year period, through 1986, to collect information

---

[4]Another longitudinal panel, the National Education Longitudinal Study (NELS:88), has been following a cohort of 8th graders since 1988 through 12th grade. In two years time, when data become available on this cohort's college experience, the analyses presented here could be repeated to ascertain changes over time either due to changing student characteristics or to changes in institutional environment, or other factors.

[5]Collection of the data was sponsored by the National Center for Educational Statistics (NCES), U.S. Department of Education.

on their high school experience and on their college and/or work experience in the years immediately following high school:[6]

| Survey Wave | Sophomore Cohort as | Senior Cohort as |
|---|---|---|
| Baseline, 1980 | High school sophomores | High school seniors |
| 1st follow-up, 1982 | High school seniors | College sophomores |
| 2nd follow-up, 1984 | College sophomores | College seniors |
| 3rd follow-up, 1986 | College seniors | College graduates |

The above cohorts, combined, contain observations on more than 21,000 youths who were in school in 1980 and who responded to each follow-up interview whether or not they continued their education through college, went to work, or engaged in some other activities. Of the sample, 1516 respondents were born in another country and, hence, were classified as immigrants. HSB is particularly well suited for analyzing immigrants' college-going patterns because immigrants were oversampled: The proportion of immigrants in the sample is twice as large as the proportion of immigrants in the 1980 general population age 15–17.

The 1980 baseline interview contains rich information on each respondent's high school experience and activities including academic or vocational "track" assignment; course-taking pattern, and other high school related activities; relationship with peers; attitudes toward education; college and occupational expectations; plans for college; and participation in postsecondary education by type of institution: vocational, two-year college, and four-year college. It also contains detailed information on the socioethnic characteristics of the respondent—including race/ethnicity and country of birth—and the educational, socioeconomic characteristics, and length of stay in the United States of each respondent's parents and the parental educational aspirations for their children.

The follow-up interviews at two-year intervals, in turn, provided information on each youth's high school graduation, and his/her activities during the four years following high school graduation, including participation in postsecondary education and in the labor market. Table 1.1 shows the unweighted and weighted gender and

---

[6]This study focuses on the educational experience of these youths and does not analyze their experience in the labor market.

## Table 1.1

### Gender and Ethnic Characteristics of HSB Analytical Sample

| | Native | | Immigrant | |
|---|---|---|---|---|
| | Percent Unweighted | Percent Weighted | Percent Unweighted | Percent Weighted |
| Ethnicity | | | | |
| Asian | 1.5 | .7 | 22.2 | 15.7 |
| Black | 18.2 | 11.4 | 11.1 | 11.2 |
| Hispanic | 20.6 | 10.9 | 49.4 | 31.7 |
| White | 57.6 | 76.0 | 16.0 | 40.1 |
| American Indian | 1.8 | .9 | .8 | .6 |
| Other | .1 | .1 | .4 | .7 |
| Gender | | | | |
| Female | 46.3 | 50.7 | 44.5 | 48.6 |
| Male | 53.7 | 49.3 | 55.5 | 51.4 |
| N | 19,581 | | 1,516 | |

SOURCE: "High School and Beyond."

NOTE: Totals may not add up to 100 percent because of rounding.

ethnic composition of the HSB sample by immigration status. All analyses presented in this report are based on the weighted sample.

The U.S. Census of Population and Housing provides information on whether children and youths were attending school at any time between February of the census year and the time of the interview, i.e., during the spring of each of the decennial censuses. It also contains information on their place of birth, age, race/ethnicity, educational attainment (i.e., years of schooling), and other information on themselves and their parents. This information allows us to distinguish immigrants from natives and to compute "in-school" rates at each age or level of schooling, most particularly in the early years of schooling, which are not available on the HSB data file.[7] It also allows analysis of changes in "in-school" rates over time.

Although rich in other ways, the census does not contain detailed information on course-taking patterns or college attendance of either immigrant or native students by type of institution, information which is available on the HSB data file.

---

[7]In this study, we examine participation rates in U.S. education by age of respondents. By and large, age corresponds to specific grades: 5–11, preschool to primary school; 12–14, middle school; 15–17, high school, and 18–24, college. The reader should keep in mind that some individuals may repeat grades. This issue is not examined here.

## Analytical Approach

Throughout this study, an immigrant is defined as a person born in another country, i.e., someone foreign-born. Children born in the United States of foreign-born parents are defined as native-born, as are children born in the United States of native-born parents.[8]

The term "in school" is used generically to indicate a person participating in any educational activity in any type of educational institution (high school, vocational institution, or two- or four-year college) leading to a high school diploma or a college degree. We also use measures of participation in specific types of institutions, e.g., high school, two-year college, or four-year college. These measures are clearly defined in the text when used.

Finally, we use four main race/ethnic classifications in our analyses: Asians, blacks, Hispanics, and white non-Hispanics. Sample-size limitations of the HSB data file did not allow breaking down these categories further by major country of origin. Sample size is not a constraint in the use of census data. Hence, when using the latter, we further divide Asians and Hispanics into the following subgroups: Chinese, Japanese, Korean, Filipino; other Asians (mostly southeast Asians); Mexicans; and other Hispanics (mainly from Central America). Immigrants from these different countries/regions of origin were found to perform differently in the U.S. labor market (Schoeni, McCarthy, and Vernez, 1996).

Two types of analytical techniques are used to address the research questions outlined above. Descriptive statistics and cross-tabulations are used to describe participation of immigrants and natives by racial/ethnic groups at various stages of the educational process and to describe the course-taking pattern and college preparation of immigrants and natives in high school (Chapters Two to Five). In Chapter Six, multivariate techniques were used to analyze the factors associated with graduation from high school and participation of high school graduates in postsecondary education. Our models' specification and estimation techniques are detailed in that chapter.

---

[8]A follow-up study, now in progress, is focusing separately on the native-born children of immigrant parents.

## Limitations

In interpreting the results, the reader should keep in mind the following limitations:

First, and unless otherwise indicated, our findings are for a cohort of immigrants who were attending the nation's high schools in the early 1980s. This has two implications. First, immigrant youths who entered the country still of school age, but did not enroll in U.S. schools, are generally excluded in our analyses as are immigrants who entered at a later age and went directly to college. Second, the educational experience of earlier cohorts of immigrant youths may not necessarily represent the expected experience of current and future cohorts of immigrant youths. Not only has the number of immigrant children in the nation's high schools doubled since 1980, the students also come from an increasingly diverse cultural and language background. The ability of the schools to respond to the needs of this population and the native-born population has arguably deteriorated, as has that of postsecondary institutions (McDonnell and Hill, 1993; Benjamin et al., 1993).

Second, our study is restricted to following high school graduates for the four years immediately after graduation and hence captures their postsecondary educational experience only over that period of time. High school graduates who delayed entry into postsecondary education for more than four years after high school graduation are excluded. However, those entering postsecondary education for the first time four years after graduation are relatively small in numbers. Manski and Wise (1983) show that of a cohort who entered postsecondary education within four years of high school, 85 percent entered within a year from graduation and 94 percent within two years of graduation. Only 6 percent waited more than two years to attend. We can infer from these findings that students who delayed entry more than four years after graduation represent a small percentage of eventual participants in any postsecondary education.

Finally, all the information was self-reported by the respondents. This is a common limitation of survey data. In particular, inaccurate recollection or misinterpretation of parental attitudes or expectations may bias results in an unknown fashion. We believe that such biases are likely to be minimal because the questions in HSB requiring recollection covered a short period of time, and attitudes were assessed by reference to specific events or expectations.

## ORGANIZATION OF THE REPORT

The second chapter provides background trend information on immigrants of school and college age, their diversity, and parental socioeconomic characteristics. The third chapter discusses the participation rates of immigrants in primary and secondary education, including high school, and compares those rates to that of natives and across racial and ethnic groups. The high school college preparation of immigrants and their high school graduation rates are discussed in the fourth chapter. Results are also presented by racial/ethnic groups and in comparison to natives. Chapter Five presents our findings regarding the college participation of immigrants and natives who are high school graduates. We also explore the college choice patterns, i.e., two-year or four-year colleges, of both immigrants and natives in the aggregate and by race/ethnicity. The findings of our multivariate analyses of factors affecting immigrant high school graduation and college-going are discussed in Chapter Six. Finally, Chapter Seven discusses the findings' implications for future demand on U.S. educational institutions.

# Chapter Two

# IMMIGRANTS OF SCHOOL AND COLLEGE AGE

This chapter documents the 1970 to 1990 numerical and compositional trends in immigration to the United States of children and youths of school and college age. It also examines their family characteristics and compares them to those of their native counterparts.

## INCREASING NUMBERS

Schools and postsecondary institutions typically do not keep separate counts and records of students who are foreign-born. The best current source about trends in numbers and characteristics of children and youths of school and college age is the decennial U.S. Census, which includes demographic and socioeconomic information on both native- and foreign-born students. As Table 2.1 indicates, immigrants constitute a growing proportion of the school-age population at every level of education, most particularly the secondary and postsecondary levels. At the primary school level, there was also a significant increase in the proportion of immigrants in the 1970s, followed by stabilization in the 1980s.

At the national level, the proportion of immigrants of high school age (15–17) is still low—6 percent—but in California more than one in five persons of school age is an immigrant. California is also the residence of more than two out of five immigrants of school age (17 and under), hence, its institutions bear the bulk of the responsibility to educate new immigrants to the United States.

Table 2.1

Proportion of Immigrants, by School and College Age Groups,
1970 to 1990

| Age Group[a] (Grade) | United States | | | California | | |
|---|---|---|---|---|---|---|
| | 1970 | 1980 | 1990 | 1970 | 1980 | 1990 |
| 5–7 (K–2) | 1.2 | 2.6 | 2.6 | 2.8 | 8.9 | 8.2 |
| 8–11 (3–6) | 1.5 | 2.9 | 3.4 | 3.7 | 9.8 | 11.3 |
| 12–14 (7–10) | 1.7 | 3.4 | 4.7 | 4.4 | 10.8 | 16.1 |
| 15–17 (11–12) | 2.0 | 3.9 | 6.0 | 5.2 | 11.8 | 22.0 |
| 18–21 (undergraduate) | 2.7 | 5.0 | 8.0 | 6.3 | 14.9 | 27.5 |
| 22–24 (graduate) | 3.6 | 5.9 | 10.2 | 7.7 | 17.2 | 31.0 |

SOURCE:  1970, 1980, and 1990, Public Use Sample of the U.S. Bureau of the Census.
[a]Age is a good indicator of the school grade a student is attending for both immigrant and native children.  In the HSB, 93 percent of the students in 12th grade were evenly split between the age of 17 and 18.  The average age for immigrants was 17.7 compared to 17.5 for natives.

## IMMIGRANTS COME AT ALL AGES

The proportion of immigrants in the school-age population increases with age because larger numbers of immigrant children and youths enter when they are older.  For instance, whereas one in twenty 12–14 year olds was foreign-born in 1990, more than one in ten college-age 22–24 year olds were foreign-born.  Again, these proportions are much higher in California, where they increased from one in six, to one in three, respectively.

The effect of lateral entry of immigrants on the composition of school-age children cohorts is best seen in Table 2.2, which compares the size of the age 5–7 cohorts of natives and immigrants to that of the age 15–17 cohorts ten years later.  Whereas the sizes of the native-born cohorts remain nearly constant over the ten-year period—except for minor changes due to mortality and net in- or out-migration of natives into California—the immigrant cohorts more than doubled in size both from 1970 to 1980 and from 1980 to 1990.

For instance, during the 1980s, 34,700 new immigrant children were added annually to the 5–7 year old cohort as it was moving from

### Table 2.2

### Aging of the Age 5–7 Cohort, by Immigration Status
(in thousands)

| Immigration Status | United States | | | California | | |
|---|---|---|---|---|---|---|
| | 1970 | 1980 | 1990 | 1970 | 1980 | 1990 |
| Immigrant | | | | | | |
| 5–7 | 150 | 250 | | 32 | 86 | |
| 15–17 | | 482 | 597 | | 145 | 250 |
| Native-born | | | | | | |
| 5–7 | 11,832 | 9,428 | | 1,123 | 886 | |
| 15–17 | | 11,991[a] | 9,393 | | 1,089 | 887 |

SOURCE: 1970, 1980, and 1990, Public Use Sample of U.S. Bureau of the Census.

[a]The increase between 1970 and 1980 in the censuses' count of that cohort cannot have actually taken place. It is most likely due to the significant improvements made in minimizing the undercount between 1970 and 1980.

primary school to middle and high school. California was the destination for nearly half of these children, 16,400 a year.

## A DIVERSE GROUP

School-age immigrants are a diverse and changing group. Table 2.3 shows that the proportion of white immigrant youths of high school age declined from one in two in 1970 to one in seven in 1990. In the meantime, the proportion of Asians increased rapidly from one in twenty to nearly one in three. Hispanics already represented a significant proportion—more than one-third—of the high-school-age immigrant population in 1970. That proportion continued to increase, however, through the 1970s and 1980s, so that by 1990 one out of two high-school-age immigrants was Hispanic. Trends have been similar in California, only more pronounced. There, nearly one out of two high-school-age immigrants was Hispanic as early as 1970. That proportion increased in the 1970s to nearly two out of every three immigrant youths and then remained at that level in the 1980s. In contrast, Asians increased their share from one out of five students in 1980 to one out of three, and whites steadily decreased theirs to less than one out of ten by 1990.

Table 2.3

**Distribution of High School Age Youths Age 15–17, by Immigration Status and Race/Ethnicity, 1970 to 1990**

| Immigration Status and Race/Ethnicity | United States | | | California | | |
|---|---|---|---|---|---|---|
| | 1970 | 1980 | 1990 | 1970 | 1980 | 1990 |
| Immigrant (N) | 233,000 | 481,640 | 597,238 | 57,100 | 145,340 | 250,143 |
| Asian | 5.6 | 20.1 | 30.1 | 11.1 | 23.4 | 31.3 |
| Black | 4.1 | 9.1 | 6.2 | 1.1 | 1.5 | .9 |
| Hispanic | 38.4 | 43.3 | 49.6 | 50.7 | 59.6 | 59.3 |
| White | 50.9 | 26.4 | 13.6 | 35.7 | 14.7 | 8.1 |
| Other | .9 | 1.1 | .4 | 1.4 | .6 | .3 |
| Total | 100.0 | 100.0 | 100.0 | 100.0 | 100.0 | 100.0 |
| Native (N) | 11,462,150 | 11,990,540 | 9,392,927 | 1,043,050 | 1,089,340 | 886,897 |
| Asian | .6 | .7 | 1.5 | 1.8 | 2.7 | 5.1 |
| Black | 13.1 | 14.5 | 15.5 | 8.0 | 10.8 | 10.0 |
| Hispanic | 4.2 | 6.4 | 8.8 | 12.4 | 18.8 | 27.5 |
| White | 81.6 | 77.6 | 73.1 | 77.3 | 66.4 | 56.3 |
| Other | .5 | .9 | 1.1 | .6 | 1.3 | 1.1 |
| Total | 100.0 | 100.0 | 100.0 | 100.0 | 100.0 | 100.0 |
| All (N) | 11,695,150 | 12,472,180 | 9,990,165 | 1,100,150 | 1,234,680 | 1,137,040 |
| Asian | .7 | 1.4 | 3.2 | 2.3 | 5.2 | 10.9 |
| Black | 12.9 | 14.3 | 14.9 | 7.5 | 9.7 | 7.9 |
| Hispanic | 4.9 | 7.8 | 11.3 | 14.4 | 23.6 | 34.5 |
| White | 81.0 | 75.6 | 69.5 | 75.1 | 60.3 | 45.7 |
| Other | .5 | .9 | 1.1 | .6 | 1.2 | .9 |
| Total | 100.0 | 100.0 | 100.0 | 100.0 | 100.0 | 100.0 |

SOURCE: 1970, 1980, and 1990 Public Use Sample of the U.S. Census Bureau.
NOTE: Percentages may not add up to totals because of rounding.

Table 2.3 also shows that immigration growth over the past 20 years has had a significant effect on the composition of the native-born population, which includes children born in the United States to immigrant parents, and hence U.S. citizens. This effect is most visible for Hispanics who have more than doubled their share in the high-school-age native cohort—from 4 to 9 percent nationwide, and from 12 to 28 percent in California. Asians have also increased their proportion among natives, but because Asian immigration is more recent than Hispanic, its effect has yet to be fully felt in the high schools of America. The growth in numbers of young immigrants and children born to immigrants has had a dramatic and cumulative effect on the current composition of school- and college-age children and youths. Again, Table 2.3 shows that whereas fewer than one in five high-school-age youths was "minority" in 1970, today about one in three is "minority." In today's California, no one racial/ethnic group represents a majority of the high-school-age cohort. These trends are expected to continue, because immigration is continuing at historically high levels.[1]

Changes in racial/ethnic composition reflect only one dimension of changes in diversity of the school-age population. Within any one group, there are changes in region/country of origin. For instance, increased immigration from Southeast Asia is changing the character of Asian immigration, which initially was more heavily Chinese, Japanese, Filipino, and more recently Korean. So it is with Hispanic immigration, although to a lesser degree. Hispanic immigration continues to be predominantly of Mexican origin, but immigration from Central America has been on the increase.

## SELECTED FAMILY CHARACTERISTICS

Culturally and linguistically diverse, school-age immigrants are also diverse in the characteristics of families they grow up in. Table 2.4 focuses on just two of those characteristics—income and the educational level of parents. It has been well established that these two family characteristics are associated with educational achievements of students in U.S. schools.

In 1990, nationwide as well as in California, immigrant youths were twice as likely as natives to be in families whose income is in the lowest quartile and three times more likely to have parents with less than 12 years of schooling. Although the relative difference between immigrants and natives varies within each racial/ethnic group, it is always in the same direction. The only exception is among blacks, where immigrants are less likely than natives to live in lower-quartile-income families and less likely to have both parents without 12 years of schooling.

---

[1]Congress is currently considering legislation that would reduce legal immigration from a current 800,000 a year to between 300,000 and 550,000. The latter is roughly equal to the number of new legal immigrants who entered the country every year throughout the 1980s. Hence, we can expect immigration to continue at least at the high levels of the 1980s for years to come.

Table 2.4

**Percentage of Youths Age 15–17 Living in Families with Income in Lowest Quartile and with Two "High School Drop-Out" Parents, by Immigration Status and Race/Ethnicity, 1990**

| Race/Ethnicity | United States | | California | |
|---|---|---|---|---|
| | Native | Immigrant | Native | Immigrant |
| Percent in Families with Income in Lowest quartile | | | | |
| Asians | 9 | 27 | 11 | 35 |
| Blacks | 48 | 32 | 40 | 41 |
| Hispanics | 36 | 45 | 31 | 46 |
| Whites | 16 | 26 | 14 | 32 |
| All | 23 | 37 | 21 | 41 |
| Percent in Families with Two Parents Having Less Than 12 Years of Schooling | | | | |
| Asians | 6 | 23 | 5 | 25 |
| Blacks | 24 | 19 | 11 | 11 |
| Hispanics | 41 | 68 | 40 | 70 |
| Whites | 8 | 21 | 4 | 17 |
| All | 13 | 43 | 15 | 50 |

SOURCE: 1990 Public Use Sample of the U.S. Census Bureau.

Of the racial/ethnic groups, Asians and whites are least likely to live in families with low income and low levels of parental education. Blacks, either native or immigrant, are significantly more likely than Asians and whites to live in low-income families and native blacks are also more likely to have parents with low levels of education. As noted above, black immigrants have parents with levels of education comparable to those of Asians and whites.

Hispanics fare the worst on parental education. Two in five native youths of Hispanic origin have less-educated parents—many of whom are immigrants—and three in four immigrant youths have such parents. But even though Hispanic natives' parental education is less than it is for blacks, their incomes are not as low as those of blacks. This is in part because Hispanic families are more likely to have two wage earners than black families.

# Chapter Three

# PARTICIPATION OF IMMIGRANT CHILDREN IN K–12

Immigrant children may enter the United States at any age. Some enter with their parents while they are still of preschool age and hence have all of their schooling in this country. But most come to the United States after having had some schooling in their country of origin and they may or may not pursue their education in a U.S. school. We might expect that the younger an immigrant is at entry the more likely she/he is to go to school here. But older children, e.g., those 16 or above, may bypass schooling in the United States altogether, most particularly if they had already left school in their home country or if they are required to work to maintain themselves and their families. These issues are explored in this chapter.[1]

## PRIMARY TO MIDDLE SCHOOL

Up to the level of middle school, immigrants are nearly as likely to be enrolled in school as natives in the same age groups. Table 3.1 indicates that in 1990, 94 percent of immigrants in the age 8–11 and age 12–14 groups nationwide were in school compared to 96 percent for natives.[2] In the earlier age 4–7 group, the proportion of children in school is lower for both groups: 74 and 71 percent, respectively. The pattern is similar in California, although the differential between

---

[1]All data analyzed in this chapter were derived from the U.S. Census of Population and Housing.

[2]Includes persons who responded yes to the census question of whether they have "attended regular school or college, including nursery school, kindergarten, elementary school, and schooling which leads to a high school diploma or a college degree."

Table 3.1

In-School Participation Rates, by Age and Immigration
Status, 1980 to 1990

| | 1980 | | 1990 | |
|---|---|---|---|---|
| Age | Native | Immigrant | Native | Immigrant |
| United States | | | | |
| 5–7 | 79 | 79 | 74 | 71 |
| 8–11 | 99 | 97 | 96 | 94 |
| 12–14 | 99 | 97 | 97 | 94 |
| 15–17 | 92 | 84 | 93 | 87 |
| California | | | | |
| 5–7 | 93 | 89 | 86 | 81 |
| 8–11 | 99 | 97 | 96 | 92 |
| 12–14 | 99 | 97 | 97 | 94 |
| 15–17 | 92 | 80 | 94 | 84 |

SOURCE: 1980 and 1990 Public Use Sample of the U.S. Bureau of
the Census.

immigrants and natives is slightly larger: three percentage points
lower compared to two, nationwide.

Over time, school enrollment rates have declined for both immigrants and natives, although the decline has been slightly larger for
the first group. For instance, for the age 8–11 group, participation
declined by 3 percent from 99 percent in 1980 for natives and also by
3 percent from 97 percent for immigrants. This decline may be par-
tially explained by an increase in the number of parents teaching
their children at home. However, whether this reason also applies to
immigrants is unknown.

## HIGH SCHOOL

Immigrants of high school age (15–17) were significantly less likely to
be in school than were natives both in 1980 and in 1990. In the latter
year, 87 percent of immigrants were in school compared to 93 percent of natives. In California, the differential is even larger: 84 percent compared to 94 percent. Contrary to the pattern noted above
for earlier ages, in-school participation of both immigrants and natives has increased between 1980 and 1990. The increase was somewhat larger for immigrants than for natives. These increases are

consistent with the outreach efforts made throughout the 1980s to reduce early-drop-out rates.

Nearly all the differential in high school participation rates between immigrants and natives is accounted for by immigrants from Mexico. Table 3.2 shows that in-school participation rates for Asian, black, and white immigrants and natives were similar both in 1980 and in 1990 and both nationwide and in California. Not so for Hispanics. Although, native Hispanic participation rates were only slightly lower than for native Asians and whites and similar to blacks, they were much lower for Hispanic immigrants, most specifically immigrants from Mexico. In 1990 as in 1980, one in four immigrants from Mexico in the 15–17 age group was not in school. In 1990, their in-school rate was nearly 20 percent lower than that of any other immigrant group and 17 percent lower than for natives of Mexican origin.

Such large disparities for just one group of immigrants raise the question of whether these youths are drop-outs from U.S. schools or instead are youths who never entered the U.S. school system in the first place. Whether the first or the second explanation prevails is critical for two reasons. First, the number of such youths is relatively large at any one point in time: 37,000 nationwide and 25,000 in California. Over time, the number of such youths becoming adults lacking a high school education will amount to hundreds of thousands.

Table 3.2

In-School Participation Rates of High School Youths Age 15–17,
by Immigration Status and Race/Ethnicity, 1990

| Race/Ethnicity | United States | | California | |
|---|---|---|---|---|
| | Native | Immigrant | Native | Immigrant |
| Asian | 95 | 94 | 96 | 95 |
| Chinese, Japanese, Korean, Filipino | 96 | 95 | 97 | 95 |
| Other Asian | 95 | 94 | 95 | 95 |
| Blacks | 91 | 91 | 91 | 93 |
| Hispanic | 91 | 83 | 93 | 77 |
| Mexican | 91 | 74 | 93 | 74 |
| Other Hispanic | 90 | 88 | 94 | 88 |
| White | 93 | 92 | 95 | 94 |

SOURCE: 1990 Public Use Sample of the U.S. Bureau of the Census.

And their prospects for success in the U.S. labor market are low (Schoeni, McCarthy, and Vernez, 1996). Second, it is critical to determine whether and how to intervene. If these youths are actually drop-outs from U.S. schools, targeted drop-out prevention programs might help address this problem. But if these youths never "drop in," efforts would need to be directed at overcoming barriers that prevent them from enrolling in school in the first place.

We suspect that the primary reason for low in-school participation rates among Mexican immigrant youths of high school age is that they do not enter the U.S. school system in the first place. On the average, Mexican immigrants have completed seven years of schooling. By the age of 15, the average Mexican has been out of school for two years. It should not be surprising, then, that a substantial proportion of Mexican youths who may enter the United States as immigrants at age 15 or above may simply choose not to enter schools here either by choice, because of inability to catch up with others their age or their native and other immigrant counterparts who have benefited from uninterrupted schooling either here or abroad, or by economic necessity because they must support themselves and their families.

There is some evidence in the literature in support of the hypothesis that some children never "drop in." In their case studies of six school districts and 49 schools within those districts, McDonnell and Hill (1993) write that:

> educators in all the districts we studied reported that schools have great difficulty reaching and holding older students who enter school several years behind. They experience school as a struggle to catch up with courses that are continually moving faster than they can. Students who come from poor areas of their source countries often come from families that expect young people to abandon school in their teens to begin work and marriage. Many see the wages available even in dead-end U.S. jobs as being highly attractive, and some must take any available work to support their brothers and sisters (pp. 72–73).

Further evidence that many immigrant youths never "drop in" is provided in Table 3.3. It shows 1990s' in-school participation rates separately for three ages: 15, 16, and 17. Participation rates are high and about the same for 15 and 16 year olds and exhibits a modest decline for 17 year olds for all immigrants of all racial/ethnic

## Table 3.3

## In-School Participation Rates of High School Age Youths, by Age and Immigration Status, Nationwide, 1990

| Race/Ethnicity | Native | | | Immigrant | | |
|---|---|---|---|---|---|---|
| | 15 | 16 | 17 | 15 | 16 | 17 |
| United States | | | | | | |
| Asian | | | | | | |
| Chinese, Japanese, | | | | | | |
| Korean, Filipino | 97 | 96 | 95 | 96 | 96 | 94 |
| Other Asian | 98 | 96 | 86 | 97 | 95 | 94 |
| Black | 94 | 92 | 86 | 96 | 94 | 84 |
| Hispanic | | | | | | |
| Mexican | 95 | 91 | 85 | 85 | 79 | 62 |
| Other Hispanic | 95 | 91 | 86 | 92 | 89 | 82 |
| White | 96 | 94 | 90 | 96 | 94 | 87 |
| All | 96 | 93 | 89 | 92 | 89 | 79 |
| California | | | | | | |
| Asian | | | | | | |
| Chinese, Japanese, | | | | | | |
| Korean, Filipino | 96 | 97 | 97 | 98 | 95 | 93 |
| Other Asian | 98 | 94 | 92 | 96 | 95 | 95 |
| Black | 94 | 92 | 88 | 95 | 95 | 91 |
| Hispanic | | | | | | |
| Mexican | 95 | 94 | 88 | 85 | 77 | 62 |
| Other Hispanic | 96 | 96 | 89 | 92 | 89 | 82 |
| White | 96 | 95 | 92 | 96 | 94 | 92 |
| All | 96 | 95 | 91 | 91 | 86 | 77 |

SOURCE: 1990 Public Use Sample of the U.S. Bureau of the Census.

groups with the marked exception of Hispanics, and most especially Mexican immigrants. For the latter, the in-school rate is already low at age 15 and decreases disproportionately (relative to other immigrants) at age 16. By age 17, fewer than two in three Mexican immigrants were in school in 1990—a rate that is more than 25 percent lower than for white, Asian, and black immigrants.

The pattern among natives differs significantly from that of immigrants. Natives of Hispanic origin have similar participation rates to Asians, blacks, and whites up to age 16. However, they as well as black natives experience a somewhat larger decline in in-school participation at age 17 than Asians and whites.

# Chapter Four

# IMMIGRANT YOUTHS IN HIGH SCHOOL: BETTER PREPARED FOR COLLEGE

How do immigrants who actually enroll in U.S. high schools actually perform? In this chapter, we address this question using data from "High School and Beyond."[1] Our focus is on those activities that are preparatory and/or consistent with eventually pursuing a college education. The college preparation of immigrants in high school is compared across racial/ethnic groups and to natives.

College preparation of high school students has many dimensions: academic, extracurricular, and motivational. Data limitations do not allow us to explore exhaustively all of these dimensions. Here we explore three of them: (1) course-taking patterns, (2) the meeting of college-entry requirements, and (3) motivations. Each of these dimensions are measured by several indicators:

- Course-taking patterns
  — "Academic track"
  — Years of math and English courses
  — Advanced placement courses

- College requirements
  — SAT or ACT test
  — Graduation from high school

---

[1]See Chapter One for a description of these data and the limitations. HSB is based on a national sample; it did not allow examining separately patterns for California or any other state. Nor did it allow separating Asians and Hispanics into subgroups.

- Attitudes toward education and college aspirations
  — Likes to work hard in school
  — Interested in school
  — Plans to go to college
  — Some college is least amount of schooling would be satisfied with
  — Would be disappointed if did not graduate from college

Being on an academic track and taking advanced placement courses are important indicators not only of intent but of capabilities of eventually pursuing a postsecondary education. Also, students on an academic track are more than three times as likely to eventually complete a bachelor's degree than students in a "general" or "vocational" track (U.S. Department of Education Statistics, 1993, Table 301). Graduation from high school and taking the SAT (or ACT) are two "gatekeeping" hurdles that must be overcome to eventually pursue a college education. Finally, whether a student plans to go to college, as well as is motivated to do so, has been found to be associated with eventual college-going.

## COURSE-TAKING PATTERN

Immigrant high school students are more likely than natives to be following an academic track and a course-taking pattern that is conducive to the eventual pursuit of a college education. Table 4.1 shows a course-taking pattern in which a higher percentage of immigrants than native students were enrolled in an academic track, took more than three years of English and math, and took advanced placement courses in algebra, geometry, trigonometry, calculus, physics, and chemistry. This pattern is consistent whether we compare natives to immigrants as a whole or whether we compare immigrants and natives across ethnic groups. And it is statistically significant: The probability that it could happen by chance alone is less than 2 percent.

Some of the differences between immigrants and natives are particularly striking. Nearly one in two immigrant students was following an academic track compared to two in five for natives. They were also 34 percent more likely to have taken three years or more of

Table 4.1

**Percentage of Students on an Academic Track and Taking Advanced Placement Courses in High School, by Race/Ethnicity and Immigration Status**

| | All | | Ethnic Groups | | | | | | | |
| | | | Asian | | Black | | Hispanic | | White | |
| | Native | Immi-grant | Native | Immi-grant | Native | Immi-grant | Native | Immi-grant | Native | Immi-grant |
|---|---|---|---|---|---|---|---|---|---|---|
| Academic track | 41 | 47 | 58 | 59 | 37 | 46 | 28 | 40 | 44 | 48 |
| Completed courses | | | | | | | | | | |
| 3+ years of English | 74 | 71 | 79 | 72 | 74 | 73 | 67 | 65 | 76 | 78 |
| 3+ years of math | 31 | 41 | 46 | 54 | 33 | 42 | 22 | 32 | 32 | 45 |
| Advanced courses | | | | | | | | | | |
| Algebra 2 | 50 | 63 | 75 | 76 | 42 | 59 | 33 | 53 | 54 | 65 |
| Geometry | 57 | 66 | 78 | 78 | 39 | 57 | 35 | 49 | 62 | 73 |
| Trigonometry | 27 | 38 | 48 | 54 | 15 | 30 | 13 | 26 | 31 | 43 |
| Calculus | 9 | 12 | 18 | 25 | 4 | 14 | 5 | 7 | 11 | 14 |
| Physics | 21 | 33 | 37 | 49 | 18 | 33 | 15 | 24 | 22 | 35 |
| Chemistry | 39 | 50 | 57 | 63 | 29 | 58 | 25 | 35 | 42 | 52 |

SOURCE: "High School and Beyond."

NOTE: The probability that a higher proportion of immigrants than natives taking the courses listed could occur by chance alone is less than 2 percent.

mathematics and more likely to have completed advanced courses in algebra, geometry, and calculus. The magnitude of the differences between immigrants and natives increases with the degree of difficulty of the math course. Whereas immigrants were 24 percent more likely than natives to take Algebra 2, they were 41 percent and 29 percent more likely to take trigonometry and calculus, respectively.

Just as immigrant youths in the nation's high schools were more likely to take advanced math courses, they were also more likely to take advanced science courses. They were 57 percent more likely to have taken an advanced physics course and 28 percent more likely to have taken an advanced chemistry course.

The only exception in this favorable course-taking pattern concerns English. Immigrants were slightly less likely to have taken three years of English courses than natives, but the difference is relatively small.

The relationship between immigrants and natives within ethnic groups is also nearly always in the same direction: Immigrants are always more likely than natives from their same ethnic group to have been on an academic track and to have taken advanced placement courses. The largest relative difference between natives and immigrants is encountered among Hispanics and the smallest among Asians.

However, there are significant variations in course-taking patterns across ethnic groups, holding immigration status constant. Again, Hispanics were the least likely of any racial/ethnic group to be placed on an academic track, to take three years of English or math, or to take advanced courses of any kind. The differences were particularly pronounced for native Hispanics: They were 50 percent (or more) less likely to be on an academic track than white and Asian natives, to have taken at least three years of math, or to have taken advanced math. Hispanic immigrants were also less likely to have taken college "gatekeeper" courses than their white and Asian counterparts, but the differences were not as large.

Blacks were somewhat less likely than whites and Asians to have taken college "gatekeeper" courses, but the differences were smaller than for Hispanics, ranging from a 16 percent lower likelihood of being on an academic track to a high 37 percent lower likelihood of having taken advanced geometry.

## MEETING COLLEGE REQUIREMENTS

Immigrant high school sophomores were no less likely than natives to have graduated from high school within four years from their sophomore year.[2] Table 4.2 shows that 81 percent of immigrant students had graduated compared to 84 percent for natives; this difference is not statistically significant.

Table 4.2 also shows differences in high school graduation rates between immigrants and natives by ethnic groupings. Within these groupings, these differences were generally small and none are significant.

Holding immigration status constant—looking down the columns in Table 4.2—the variations of graduation rates across racial/ethnic groups are similar to those noted above for course-taking patterns. Asians and whites were the most likely to graduate from high school whether native or foreign-born. Hispanics were least likely to graduate, with one out of four failing to complete high school within two years of their senior year. These ethnic differences have been well

### Table 4.2

### Percentage of 1980 High School Sophomores Who Graduated from High School by Summer 1982, by Immigration Status, Race/Ethnicity, and Gender

|                 | Native | Immigrant |
|-----------------|--------|-----------|
| All             | 83     | 81        |
| Ethnicity       |        |           |
| Asian           | 86     | 95        |
| Black           | 79     | 72        |
| Hispanic        | 75     | 70        |
| White and other | 85     | 87        |

SOURCE: "High School and Beyond."
NOTE: None of the differences between natives and immigrants shown in this table are statistically significant.

---

[2]The graduation rate was measured two years from the year in which he/she would have normally graduated. Even though 17 percent of sophomores did not complete high school within those two years, almost half of these eventually received a high school degree or an equivalency certificate within six years of their sophomore year (Ogle and Alsalam, 1990, p. 20).

documented in previous research (Koretz, 1990). What our results add to previous findings is that these racial/ethnic differences remain when we separate immigrants from natives.

Many colleges, most particularly four-year colleges and universities, also require applicants to take either the SAT or ACT. Here again, immigrant students are just as likely to take these tests as natives, regardless of racial/ethnic grouping (Table 4.3).

## ATTITUDES AND EXPECTATIONS

The information collected in "High School and Beyond" offers an opportunity to compare the attitudes toward education and the college aspirations of high school students and their parents. It clearly shows that immigrant students have more positive views toward schooling and have higher aspirations for a college education than natives (Table 4.4).[3]

Two out of three immigrant youths reported that "they liked working hard in school" compared to one in two natives. Similarly, they were 7 and 12 percent more likely to "plan to go to college" and "to expect to be disappointed should they fail to graduate from college" than their native counterparts, respectively. The probability that the consistent pattern of differences between immigrants and natives exhibited in Table 4.4 could happen by chance alone is less than 2 percent.

The higher educational aspirations of immigrants hold within each racial/ethnic group; the differences are particularly large between Hispanic immigrants and Hispanic natives. The first were 29 percent more likely than the second to report positive attitudes and high expectations for postsecondary education. Where educational expectations and "working hard" to fulfill them are concerned, Hispanic immigrants are generally similar to immigrants from other ethnic groups. These relative aspirations, however, are not maintained among Hispanic natives, who have the lowest ratings on indicators of college aspirations.

---

[3]In Chapter Six, we examine whether these attitudes and aspirations are associated with participation in postsecondary education.

Table 4.3

Percentage of High School Students Taking the ACT or SAT Tests, by Race/Ethnicity and Immigration Status

| | Ethnic Groups | | | | | | | | | |
| | All | | Asian | | Black | | Hispanic | | White | |
| | Native | Immi-grant | Native | Immi-grant | Native | Immi-grant | Native | Immi-grant | Native | Immi-grant |
|---|---|---|---|---|---|---|---|---|---|---|
| Took SAT or ACT | 46 | 46 | 50 | 53 | 37 | 34 | 30 | 38 | 49 | 52 |

Table 4.4

Percentage of High School Seniors with Selected Attitudes Toward Postsecondary Education, by Race/Ethnicity and Immigration Status

| | Ethnic Groups | | | | | | | | | |
| | All | | Asian | | Black | | Hispanic | | White | |
| | Native | Immi-grant | Native | Immi-grant | Native | Immi-grant | Native | Immi-grant | Native | Immi-grant |
|---|---|---|---|---|---|---|---|---|---|---|
| Attitudes toward education | | | | | | | | | | |
| Likes to work hard in school | 52 | 62 | 63 | 66 | 69 | 70 | 53 | 68 | 50 | 56 |
| Interested in school | 74 | 78 | 83 | 77 | 85 | 79 | 74 | 86 | 73 | 74 |
| College aspirations | | | | | | | | | | |
| Plans to go to college | 66 | 73 | 83 | 84 | 67 | 66 | 67 | 72 | 67 | 72 |
| Some college is least amount of schooling would be satisfied with | 48 | 57 | 43 | 50 | 43 | 60 | 47 | 71 | 50 | 54 |
| Would be disappointed if not college graduate | 56 | 68 | 72 | 78 | 61 | 61 | 45 | 74 | 57 | 64 |

SOURCE: "High School and Beyond."
NOTE: The probability that the pattern of differences between immigrants and natives shown in this table could have occurred by chance alone is less than 2 percent.

The immigrant parents of immigrant children also hold higher college expectations for their children than native parents, mirroring those of their children.  Table 4.5 shows that immigrant parents are more likely to plan for and want their children to go to college after high school.  For instance, 71 percent of immigrant mothers want their children to go to college compared to 60 percent for native mothers.  This pattern holds for fathers as well and across racial/ethnic groupings.  As in all other aspects of preparation for college considered in this chapter, Hispanic native-born parents have the lowest aspirations of any group.[4]

## CONCLUSIONS

Academic and motivational preparation for college begins early in primary and secondary school and is particularly important at the high school level.  We found that in key aspects of preparation for college, immigrants were more likely to make choices consistent with eventual college-going than their native counterparts, regardless of race or ethnicity.  They were more likely to follow an academic track, take advanced courses in math and science, take the SAT or ACT, and plan to go to college and work hard to achieve their expectations.

There are variations among immigrants of different ethnic groups just as there are variations among natives of different ethnic groups. Asian immigrants generally performed better on indicators of preparation for college, followed by white and black immigrants.  Hispanic immigrants performed the lowest on nearly all indicators of college preparation except motivation and expectations.  This pattern among immigrants of different ethnicity is similar to the pattern encountered among natives of different ethnic groups.  Native Hispanics score the lowest of any group on indicators of college aspirations.

---

[4]These findings are consistent with recent ones from a survey of 189 adolescent students in Mexico and the United States conducted by Marcelo and Carola Suárez-Orozco and reported in the *L.A. Times*, February 22, 1996.  They found that Mexican immigrants valued schooling more than second-generation Mexicans.  The significant lowering in expectations between Hispanic immigrant youths (and their parents) and Hispanic native youths (and their parents) merits further investigation to determine what may be causing it.  Understanding this may be key to helping Hispanics increase their educational attainment.  See also Suárez-Orozco and Suárez-Orozco (1995).

Table 4.5

Percentage of High School Seniors Whose Parents Have Selected Expectations

| | All | | Asian | | Black | | Hispanic | | White | |
| | Native | Immi-grant | Native | Immi-grant | Native | Immi-grant | Native | Immi-grant | Native | Immi-grant |
|---|---|---|---|---|---|---|---|---|---|---|
| College is father's after-high-school plan for respondent | 53 | 62 | 73 | 79 | 44 | 52 | 37 | 49 | 56 | 68 |
| Mother wants respondent to go to college | 60 | 70 | 80 | 84 | 60 | 66 | 45 | 64 | 62 | 72 |

SOURCE: "High School and Beyond."

# Chapter Five

# PARTICIPATION IN POSTSECONDARY EDUCATION

Even though we have shown in Chapter Four that a high proportion of immigrant high school students take college "gatekeeping" courses and aspire to pursue a postgraduate education, this may not necessarily mean that they actually continue their education at higher rates. Financial constraints—such as lower access to scholarships and loans—as well as other family and institutional factors may limit their access to postsecondary education in the United States.

In this chapter, we examine the extent to which immigrants who graduated from U.S. high schools pursued a postsecondary education. We find that, overall, immigrant graduates of U.S. high schools were more likely to pursue postsecondary studies in the United States than natives. In the next chapter, we explore the family and individual factors that are associated with these higher college-going rates.

## COLLEGE-GOING RATES OF HIGH SCHOOL GRADUATES

No one measure of participation in postsecondary education can capture the full range of college-going patterns that might be followed by immigrant and native high school graduates. Hence, we used three measures of participation to ascertain whether they provide a consistent view of immigrants' postsecondary experience relative to those of natives:

- **Any postsecondary education:** the proportion of *high school graduates* who enrolled in any post-high school education (including trade or technical school) for any length of time during the four years following graduation from high school.

- **Any college:** the proportion of *high school graduates* who enrolled in either a two- or four-year college for any length of time during the four years following graduation from high school.

- **At least 42 months of college:** the proportion of *high school graduates* who remained in college for at least 42 months in the four years following their high school senior year.[1]

These measures were computed from "High School and Beyond," and hence, for the same students who were in high school in Chapter Four.[2] The period covered is 1980 through 1984 for the senior cohort and 1982 through 1986 for the sophomore cohort. As a check of consistency, we also used the 1980 census to compute the in-school enrollment rate of *high school graduates* age 18–21. This rate is not directly comparable to the postsecondary attendance rates derived from "High School and Beyond." It measures school attendance from February 1, 1980 or 1990, to the time of the census interview in the spring of that year; it is a shorter period than the four-year period used for the HSB measures. The census measure includes "only schooling which leads to a high school diploma (including GED) or a college degree"—as does the HSB's "any college" measure. Although we would expect the value of the census measure to be lower than that of the HSB measure, we would expect any differentials between immigrants and natives to be in the same direction and roughly in the same order of magnitude.

Figure 5.1 indicates that all four measures of postsecondary participation of immigrant and native high school graduates go in the same direction: Immigrants were more likely than natives to enroll in postsecondary education, attend college, and stay continuously through four years of college. All differences are statistically significant at the 1 percent level. The differential between immigrants and natives is the largest for our measure of college "continuance":

---

[1]An indicator of uninterrupted continuous college attendance.

[2]Unless otherwise noted, all figures presented in this chapter were derived from "High School and Beyond."

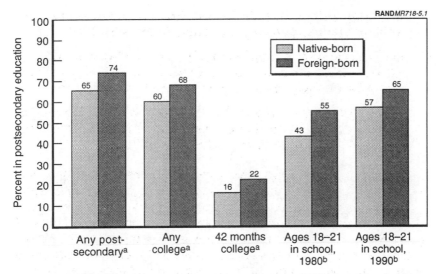

SOURCES: "High School and Beyond" and 1980 and 1990 Public Use Sample of the U.S. Bureau of the Census.

NOTE: All rates are conditional on high school graduation. See text for definition of the various participation rates.

[a]Calculated using "High School and Beyond."

[b]Calculated using the 1980 and 1990 Public Use Sample of the U.S Bureau of the Census.

**Figure 5.1—Participation Rates of High School Graduates in Postsecondary Education, by Immigration Status**

Immigrants were 33 percent more likely than natives to remain continuously through four years of college immediately following high school graduation.[3]

As noted above, these differential rates prevailed in the early part of the 1980s. Since then, immigration has not only increased but has also changed in composition (see Chapter Two). To assess whether those trends have affected postsecondary participation rates, Figure

---

[3]These findings are consistent with Rumbaut (1995). Studying a sample of 15,000 high school students in the San Diego Unified School District in 1986 and 1989, he concluded that "educational achievement, as measured by GPA, appears to decline from the first to the second and third generations" (pp. 37–38).

5.1 also displays the 1990 census in-school rate for 18–21 year old high school graduates. In-school rates increased for both immigrants and natives during the 1980–1990 decade, but 1990 immigrants age 18–21 continued to have higher in-school rates than natives.

Table 5.1 indicates that the higher rates of participation in postsecondary education by immigrant high school graduates hold within each racial and ethnic group.[4] Holding immigration status constant,

Table 5.1

**Percentage of High School Graduates Participating in Postsecondary Education, by Immigration Status and Race/Ethnicity**

| | Participation Rates in | | | | | |
|---|---|---|---|---|---|---|
| | Any Postsecondary Education | | 2- and 4-Year College | | At Least 42 Months of College | |
| | Native | Immigrant | Native | Immigrant | Native | Immigrant |
| All | 65 | 74 | 60 | 68 | 16 | 22 |
| Ethnicity | | | | | | |
| Asian | 81 | 86 | 79 | 84 | 33 | 29 |
| Black | 62 | 73 | 55 | 59 | 11 | 17 |
| Hispanic | 52 | 70 | 45 | 65 | 8 | 18 |
| White | 67 | 72 | 62 | 67 | 18 | 23 |

| | In-School Rates of 18–21 year olds | | | |
|---|---|---|---|---|
| | 1980 | | 1990 | |
| | Native | Immigrant | Native | Immigrant |
| All | 43 | 55 | 57 | 65 |
| Asian | 67 | 68 | 77 | 82 |
| Japanese, Chinese, Korean, Filipino | 70 | 71 | 82 | 81 |
| Other Asians | 40 | 65 | 67 | 83 |
| Black | 40 | 57 | 50 | 66 |
| Hispanic | 38 | 50 | 54 | 50 |
| Mexican | 35 | 33 | 53 | 44 |
| Other Hispanic | 42 | 57 | 56 | 58 |
| White | 43 | 54 | 59 | 67 |

SOURCES: "High School and Beyond" for measures in the top part of the table and 1980 and 1990 Public Use Sample of the U.S. Census Bureau for measures in the bottom part of the table.

---

[4]The only exception is that the 1980 and 1990 census in-school rates are higher for natives than for immigrants of Mexican origin. The disparity was small in 1980 (35 compared to 33 percent) but increased in 1990 (52 compared to 44 percent).

however, there are wide disparities in college-going rates among racial and ethnic groups that mirror the differentials in "college preparation" described in the previous chapter. High school graduates of Asian origin were the most likely of any racial/ethnic group to enroll in postsecondary education whether they were native or foreign-born.

About four in five Asian high school graduates went to college and nearly one in three persevered through four years of college. In contrast, about two in three white high school graduates—whether native or foreign-born—go to college with about one in five staying continuously through four years.

College-going and continuity rates of black and Hispanic immigrants were similar and only slightly lower than the rates of white immigrants. However, and confirming previous research (Koretz, 1990), black and Hispanic native high school graduates had lower college-going rates than whites, with Hispanic natives the least likely of all racial/ethnic groups to go on for four uninterrupted years of college. Less than one in two went to college and less than one in ten remained continuously through four years.

Our comparisons of changes in in-school rates between 1980 and 1990 suggest that this pattern has continued over time (see the bottom of Table 5.1) with one possible exception. Whereas in 1980, black natives had a higher in-school rate than Hispanics (as noted above), 40 compared to 37 percent, the reverse became true in 1990, 50 compared to 54 percent.

Sample-size limitations in the HSB data did not allow us to disaggregate between country of origin of immigrants. But the census data suggest that there are significant differences in college-going rates of high school graduates within a racial or ethnic group. Hispanics of Mexican origin—either native or foreign-born—are less likely than Hispanics from any other countries of origin to be in school. And Asians from Japanese, Chinese, and Filipino origin are more likely to pursue postsecondary education than Asians from other countries, primarily the countries of Southeast Asia. This is particularly the case for those U.S. natives originating from that region of the world.

## CHOICE OF INSTITUTION

Students pursuing a college education can take several paths, three of which are examined here: (1) go to a two-year college and no further; (2) go to a two-year college and then switch to a four-year college; or (3) go directly to a four-year college. The extent to which immigrants make different institutional choices from natives has bearing on the current and future demands placed on different types of educational institutions.

Table 5.2 shows the college "paths" immigrant and native students followed during the four years following their high school senior year. Immigrants were about 10 percent more likely than natives to go to two-year colleges and no further. They were also 20 percent more likely than natives to begin in a two-year college and then switch to a four-year college.

Consistent with the patterns observed in previous chapters, Hispanics, both native and immigrant, are the most likely of any racial/ethnic group to go to a two-year college and no further. Hispanic immigrants are also more likely to go to both two- and four-year institutions than any other group except Asian immigrants.

Table 5.2

Distribution of Immigrants and Natives, by Type of College Attended and Race/Ethnicity

| Type of College Attended | All | | Ethnic Groups | | | | | | | |
|---|---|---|---|---|---|---|---|---|---|---|
| | | | Asian | | Black | | Hispanic[a] | | White | |
| | Native | Immi-grant | Native | Immi-grant | Native | Immi-grant | Native | Immi-grant | Native | Immi-grant |
| Two-year college | 35 | 38 | 38 | 31 | 36 | 40 | 51 | 48 | 32 | 33 |
| Four-year college | 49 | 43 | 42 | 44 | 49 | 48 | 36 | 29 | 51 | 51 |
| Both two- and four-year college | 16 | 18 | 20 | 25 | 15 | 12 | 13 | 23 | 17 | 16 |
| Total | 100 | 100 | 100 | 100 | 100 | 100 | 100 | 100 | 100 | 100 |

SOURCE: "High School and Beyond."

[a]The differences between immigrants and natives in type of college attended are statistically significant at the 1 percent level for all students and for Hispanic students, but are not statistically significant for Asians, blacks, and whites.

# Chapter Six

# FACTORS ASSOCIATED WITH EDUCATIONAL ATTAINMENT

In the previous chapter, we showed that immigrants were as likely as natives to graduate from high school[1] and that as high school graduates they were more likely to pursue a college education than their native counterparts. In this chapter, we explore the family and individual reasons for those differentials. Specifically, we address the following questions:

- Are the differentials in educational attainment due to differences in immigration status or some other individual or family factors?

- Do different factors affect high school graduation or college-going of immigrants and of natives?

- Do different factors affect high school graduation or college-going of youths of different racial/ethnic backgrounds, regardless of immigration status?

## CONCEPTUAL FRAMEWORK

Our overall approach to analyzing how individual and family factors influence the educational achievement of immigrants and natives is illustrated in Figure 6.1. The variables chosen for inclusion in the model and the way they are organized into components are based on

---

[1]Conditional on having been in an American school by the 10th grade.

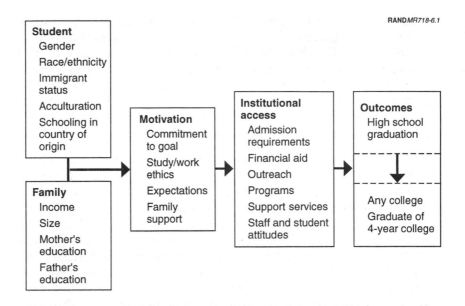

RAND*MR718-6.1*

**Figure 6.1—Conceptual Framework for Analysis of Educational
Attainment of Immigrant Youths**

the literature on immigrants' behavior, psychological well-being, and factors associated with educational achievement in the general population. By identifying the important factors and relationships, the model also helps assess the contributions of prior research to our understanding of immigrant youths' educational decisions.

The model suggests that individual and family socioeconomic characteristics, including motivation and parental expectations, combine with institutional factors—such as outreach, access, requirements, and financial and social support—in predicting immigrant and native educational attainments.

In addition to gender and race/ethnicity, found to be associated with educational achievements in previous studies (e.g., Manski and Wise, 1983; Koretz, 1990; Grissmer et al., 1994), our individual factors include immigration status and "degree of acculturation." Immigration status is included, of course, because immigrants were shown in our previous chapters to be better prepared to pursue postsecondary studies and indeed pursued such studies at higher rates. In turn, the process of acculturation to a new culture and institutional and social norms was found to lead to psychological stresses, even though a link between the latter and educational attainment has not been established (Chapter One). Learning a new language is also part of the acculturation process, and the degree to which one becomes proficient in it may in itself affect individual or institutional decisions about the pursuit of postsecondary education.

All family socioeconomic factors included in our model—family income, family size, and education of mother and father—have been found in previous research to be associated with educational attainment. Family income and size together define the financial resources that may be available to any one sibling. Family size also measures the relative distribution of parental time and attention among siblings (see Grissmer et al., 1994; Hill and O'Neill, 1993; Hanushek, 1992; Blake 1989; Wilson and Justiz, 1988; and Tracey and Sedlacek, 1985). Higher parental educational achievement has been associated with high math and verbal achievements in children (Grissmer et al., 1994) and with the provision of a more stimulating home environment (Bradley, 1985; Kohn and Schooler, 1983).

Motivation encompasses a broad set of individual and parental dispositions toward goal achievement, work ethics or study habits, and expectations about future intellectual, financial, and occupational achievements for oneself or others. Ethnographic research is replete with references to the selectivity of immigrants and the higher value some cultures place upon education, most specifically Asian cultures (see Chapter One). However, with one exception (Kao and Tienda, 1995), past research has not explored whether these predispositions are actually linked with educational attainment.

The last major component in our model includes a set of institutional factors that defines access to and support of an individual in postsecondary education. Some states have made significant investments in public higher education and offer a broad range of alternatives including community colleges, state universities, and major research universities. Availability of financial assistance is another dimension of access that has been found to be associated with college-going.[2]  And attitudes of teachers, admission personnel, and administrators toward immigrants as well as other groups may also influence college-going (see Chapter One).

## DEFINITIONS OF VARIABLES AND STATISTICAL METHODS

We used data from "High School and Beyond" to estimate the model outlined above.  The actual measures and statistical methods used are outlined below.

### Definitions of Variables

We used three outcome variables:  measures of high school graduation; participation in any college within four years from high school graduation; and continuous college attendance for four years after high school graduation.  These are the same outcome measures we discussed in Chapters Four and Five, respectively.

The independent variables actually used in our multivariate analysis are listed in Table 6.1 along with their means and standard errors for natives and immigrants.[3]  The independent variables included in our models are generally self-explanatory.  However, because of limitations in the availability of data in High School and Beyond, we used "proxy" variables to measure some of the factors included in Figure 6.1.  In the absence of a direct measure of "acculturation," it was proxied in our models by the length of time the respondent had been in the United States and by whether or not English was mostly spoken at home.  Motivation and expectations are measured by three variables: "respondent likes to work hard in school"; "mother wants youth to attend college"; and "parents always know what their child does."  The latter may be a measure of parental support or guidance of the respondent as well.

---

[2]A review of the extensive literature on the effects of student financial aid on college-going is contained in Klein et al. (1992), pp. 66–77.

[3]We checked for multicollinearity among our independent variables.  The coefficient of correlations ($R^2$) between any two independent variables was low, generally below .30.  The highest coefficient of correlations (.43) was between mother's and father's education.

Table 6.1

Weighted Means and Standard Errors for Independent Variables

| Variables | Native Mean | Native Standard Error | Immigrant Mean | Immigrant Standard Error |
|---|---|---|---|---|
| Individual Characteristics | | | | |
| 5 years or less in U.S. | | | .18 | .29 |
| 6–10 years in U.S. | | | .21 | .30 |
| Asian | .01 | .08 | .16 | .27 |
| Black | .11 | .32 | .11 | .23 |
| Hispanic | .11 | .32 | .32 | .35 |
| White | .73 | | .41 | |
| Female | .51 | .51 | .49 | .37 |
| English proficiency | .98 | .16 | .63 | .36 |
| Family Characteristics | | | | |
| Income less than $16K | .31 | .47 | .33 | .35 |
| Income more than $25K | .23 | .43 | .19 | .29 |
| No siblings | .11 | .32 | .11 | .23 |
| 3 or more siblings | .47 | .51 | .46 | .37 |
| Mother not high school graduate | .17 | .38 | .25 | .32 |
| Mother some college | .21 | .42 | .23 | .31 |
| Mother college graduate | .12 | .34 | .11 | .23 |
| Father not high school graduate | .20 | .41 | .24 | .31 |
| Father some college | .19 | .40 | .16 | .27 |
| Father college graduate | .18 | .39 | .22 | .31 |
| Mother working | .86 | .36 | .81 | .29 |
| Motivation and Expectations | | | | |
| Works hard in school | .50 | .51 | .60 | .36 |
| Mother wants youth to go to college | .36 | .51 | .65 | .35 |
| Parent always knows where youth is | .68 | .47 | .69 | .34 |
| Institutional Access | | | | |
| Lives in Northeast | .22 | .42 | .24 | .32 |
| Lives in North Central | .29 | .46 | .18 | .28 |
| Lives in West | .16 | .37 | .28 | .33 |
| Lives in rural area | .16 | .38 | .03 | .16 |
| Lives in large city | .10 | .31 | .21 | .30 |

NOTE: See Appendix A for definition of variables.

HSB contains no direct measures of access to postsecondary institutions. Hence, we control for potential access biases in our models by differentiating across the four regions of the country and for residence in rural areas and large cities, i.e., cities of 500,000 people or more.[4]

Detailed definitions for each variable and a complete display of the weighted means and standard deviations for the entire sample and for immigrants, natives, Asians, blacks, Hispanics, and whites, respectively, are summarized in Tables A-1 to A-3 in Appendix A.

## Statistical Methods

We used a linear probability model (ordinary least square (OLS)) regression method to identify the factors that were significantly related to each of our three outcome measures. The estimated coefficients resulting from this procedure can easily be interpreted: They indicate the number of percentage points added to the value of the dependent variable (the outcome) for each percentage point added to the independent variable.

We used the same full specification for each of the three outcomes and each model was estimated for the whole sample, natives only, immigrants only, Asians only, blacks only, Hispanics only, and whites only. This approach allows one to identify whether there are major differences in the relative importance of the various factors between natives and immigrants and between racial/ethnic groups.

## DISCUSSION OF RESULTS

We now turn to a discussion of the factors that our multivariate analyses found associated with high school graduation, college-going, and continuity of college attendance. Significant factors are discussed below by categories in the following order: (1) individual characteristics; (2) family characteristics; (3) motivation and parental expectations/support; and (4) institutional access. The reader is reminded that throughout this discussion, the significance and magnitude of the association between our measures of educational

---

[4]Questions of immigrant students' access to postsecondary educational institutions and these institutions' responses to growing numbers of immigrants are explored in a companion study. See Gray and Rolph (1996). Manski and Wise (1983) also used these measures to control for access in their study of college choice in America.

attainment and each specific factor are those obtained while holding all other factors constant, that is, controlling for the effect of all other factors considered in our models. All models included the same set of factors.[5]

To facilitate interpretation, the tables that follow show only the estimated coefficient of the factors that were found statistically significant at the 5 percent level or lower.[6] Each coefficient indicates the change in percentage, positive or negative, in the value of the measure of educational outcome due to a 1 percent change in the value of the factor it is associated with. Complete results of the multivariate regression models are included in Appendix B. [7]

## Individual Characteristics

In general, the rates of high school graduation, college-going, and continuity in college were found to be highest among Asians and lowest among Hispanics, holding all other factors constant. Otherwise, there are variations in the relative effect of other individual factors between natives and immigrants and between ethnic groups, as noted below (see Table 6.2).

*Immigrant status*, per se, is not associated with high school graduation or college-going, but it is positively associated with continuity

---

[5]The only exception was when a factor was irrelevant to a model. For instance, the model for "native only" does not include "immigration status" and "time in the country," because all natives are nonimmigrant by definition. For the same reason, "immigration status" is not included in the "immigrant only" model and the race/ethnicity variables are not included in the race/ethnicity-specific models.

[6]Our significance levels may be conservative because we did not correct for heteroscedasticity in the error term due to the binary nature of our variables (i.e., zero-one variables). As a result, variables that would have been significant had we corrected for heteroscedasticity may be shown as not significant in our analysis. The coefficient estimates, however, are unbiased. Also, we did not correct for potential biases due to the stratified cluster sampling method used in the HSB survey. Accounting for design effects in a regression requires the use of a simulation technique that we did not pursue. Hence, the reader should keep in mind that marginally significant results may be actually insignificant if the design effects are accounted for. Highly significant effects (1 percent or more) would, however, remain significant. The estimated regression coefficients are not affected by this issue and hence are unbiased.

[7]The technically inclined reader is referred to Appendix B for the complete regression estimates for all factors including statistically insignificant ones.

Table 6.2

**Individual Characteristics Associated with Educational Attainment, for All and by Immigration Status and Race/Ethnicity**

| | All | Native | Immi–grant | Asian | Black | His-panic | White |
|---|---|---|---|---|---|---|---|
| High School Graduates[a] | | | | | | | |
| Immigrant | | NR | NR | 5.1 | | | |
| 5 years or less in U.S. | | NR | | | 13.9 | | |
| 6–10 years in U.S. | | NR | | | | −8.4 | |
| Asian | 4.5 | | | NR | NR | NR | NR |
| Black | | | | NR | NR | NR | NR |
| Hispanic | −2.9 | −2.4 | −8.9 | NR | NR | NR | NR |
| Female | −.8 | −.8 | | | 2.3 | | −1.1 |
| English proficiency | | −3.8 | | | | 5.0 | |
| Went to Any College[b] | | | | | | | |
| Immigrant | | NR | NR | | 11.3 | 10.5 | |
| 5 years or less in U.S. | | NR | | | | −14.8 | |
| 6–10 years in U.S. | −6.4 | NR | | | −25.3 | | |
| Asian | | | +12.2 | NR | NR | NR | NR |
| Black | −.5 | | | NR | NR | NR | NR |
| Hispanic | −7.4 | −8.2 | | NR | NR | NR | NR |
| Female | 1.5 | 1.6 | | | | | |
| English proficiency | −9.2 | −11.0 | | −8.1 | | −9.3 | |
| Was in College 42 Months or More[b] | | | | | | | |
| Immigrant | 4.8 | NR | NR | | 7.5 | 10.8 | |
| 5 years or less in U.S. | | NR | | | | −10.0 | |
| 6–10 years in U.S. | −7.4 | NR | | −15.2 | | −8.5 | |
| Asian | 8.6 | +11.7 | | NR | NR | NR | NR |
| Black | −3.3 | −3.5 | | NR | NR | NR | NR |
| Hispanic | −3.5 | −3.7 | | NR | NR | NR | NR |
| Female | −1.3 | | −10.0 | | | −1.7 | |
| English proficiency | | | | | | | |

NOTE: Figures in this table were extracted from the final full regression models as shown in Appendix B. A blank indicates that the variable was included in the model but was statistically insignificant. NR means the variable was not relevant, hence not included in that particular model.

[a]Conditional on having attended 10th grade.

[b]Conditional on having graduated from high school.

of college attendance. All else being equal, immigrant status is consistently associated only with continuity of college attendance. The effect of immigration status on this latter outcome is particularly strong for blacks and Hispanics; blacks or Hispanic immigrants are 8 and 11 percent more likely, respectively, to persevere in college than

natives of the same racial/ethnic background.  For blacks and Hispanics, immigration status is also positively associated with college-
going, all else being equal.  Immigration status is not associated with
any of our measures of educational attainment for Asians and whites.

The *shorter the time* an immigrant youth has been in the United
States, the lower are her/his college-going and continuity rates.
Time in the United States, however, is not associated with high
school graduation rates.  The effect of time lived in the United States
is particularly strong for Hispanic immigrants.  A Hispanic
immigrant who has been here one to five years is 15 percent less
likely to go to college than other immigrants who have been here
longer.  The lack of association of time in the United States with
graduation from high school is most likely because our sample of
immigrants excludes anyone who was not in or was no longer in
school in 10th grade (also see Chapter Two).

*English spoken at home*, another measure of acculturation, is not associated with high school graduation or continuity in college but is
negatively associated with college-going.  We would have expected
this measure of English usage to be positively associated with
college-going.  A possible reason for the unexpected finding is that
"English spoken at home" is a poor proxy for "English proficiency" of
the student himself or herself.

All else equal, *Asian youths* are more likely to graduate from high
school and go continuously to college than any other racial/ethnic
group, whereas *Hispanic youths* are least likely to graduate from high
school and go to college.  This finding is consistent with the descriptive findings noted in previous chapters.  The positive association of
Asian background is particularly strong with college continuity—an
Asian high school graduate is 9 percent more likely than anyone else
to stay continuously in college for four years.  For Hispanics, the
negative relationship is strongest for any college-going—a Hispanic
high school graduate youth is 7 percent less likely to go to college
than anyone else.  All else being equal, blacks are no less likely to
graduate from high school than whites, but they are somewhat less
likely to stay in college continuously (3 percent less).  With regard to
college continuity, blacks are comparable to youths of Hispanic
background.

The differences between *males and females* are relatively small on all three educational outcomes considered here—they range between .8 to 1.6 percent lower—all else being equal. Female immigrants are, however, much less likely to pursue college continuously.

## Family Structure

Consistent with previous research, higher rates of high school graduation, college-going, and continuity in college are found among youths who live in families with higher incomes, have fewer siblings, have a more educated mother, or have a more educated father. This is generally the case for immigrants and natives and for all racial/ethnic groups. However, there are differences in the relative size of the effect of specific family factors among these groups (see Table 6.3).

*Low family income* is related negatively to high school graduation, college-going, and college continuity, whereas the opposite is true for high income, generally, regardless of immigration status or racial/ethnic groups. However, low income had a disproportionate negative influence on college continuity for immigrants. Low income also had a larger negative influence on Hispanics than on other racial/ethnic groups.

*Family composition* is associated with all of our three measures of outcome. Having no siblings or more than three siblings has a negative effect on all three of our measures of educational attainment for most groups. There are differences in the relative influence of these two factors between immigrants and natives—the educational attainment of the second group is more (negatively) affected by siblings. Also, the effect of these factors on blacks and whites is greater than on Hispanics and Asians.

The higher the *education* of either mother or father the higher the educational attainment of youths with such parents, regardless of immigration status or racial/ethnic group. The effect of either parents' education is larger on college-going and college continuity than on high school graduation. Also, the influence of the father's level of education is nearly always greater than the influence of the mother's level of education. This difference is larger for immigrants than natives. But the difference is reversed for blacks, for whom we found

## Table 6.3

## Family Characteristics Associated with Educational Attainment, for All and by Immigration Status and Race/Ethnicity

| | All | Native | Immi–grant | Asian | Black | His-panic | White |
|---|---|---|---|---|---|---|---|
| High School Graduates[a] | | | | | | | |
| Income less than $16K | -.9 | | | | | -5.4 | |
| Income more than $25K | 1.6 | 1.7 | | | 3.7 | 3.5 | 1.3 |
| No siblings | -4.1 | -4.3 | | | -5.8 | | -3.8 |
| 3 or more siblings | -1.7 | -1.8 | | | -2.5 | | -1.9 |
| Mother not HS graduate | -5.5 | -5.7 | | 7.5 | -4.2 | -3.7 | -6.4 |
| Mother some college | | | | 9.9 | | | |
| Mother college graduate | 1.6 | 1.7 | | | | | |
| Father not HS graduate | -1.4 | -1.5 | | -6.2 | | | -1.8 |
| Father some college | 1.6 | 1.6 | | -6.7 | | | 1.5 |
| Father college graduate | 2.4 | 2.2 | 6.4 | | | 5.7 | 2.1 |
| Mother working | -3.4 | -3.3 | -6.5 | | -2.5 | -4.9 | -3.7 |
| Went to Any College[b] | | | | | | | |
| Income less than $16K | -1.9 | -2.0 | | -.8 | -3.7 | -5.3 | -2.4 |
| Income more than $25K | 3.3 | 3.5 | | | | 4.1 | 2.8 |
| No siblings | | -1.6 | | | -5.8 | | |
| 3 or more siblings | -3.4 | -3.4 | -7.2 | | -4.1 | | -3.5 |
| Mother not HS graduate | -5.4 | -5.9 | | | | -4.2 | -6.8 |
| Mother some college | 7.0 | 7.4 | | | 12.3 | 7.1 | 6.4 |
| Mother college graduate | 10.2 | 10.7 | | | 13.1 | 14.8 | 9.6 |
| Father not HS graduate | -4.4 | -4.2 | | | | | -6.7 |
| Father some college | 8.2 | 8.1 | 12.2 | | 10.3 | 4.3 | 8.1 |
| Father college graduate | 16.0 | 16.0 | 13.5 | 11.9 | 7.9 | 18.7 | 15.8 |
| Mother working | 3.1 | 3.0 | 6.1 | | 5.7 | 6.8 | |
| Was in College 42 Months or More[b] | | | | | | | |
| Income less than $16K | -1.5 | -1.3 | -6.0 | | -.9 | | -1.9 |
| Income more than $25K | 4.4 | 4.7 | | | | 3.6 | 4.5 |
| No siblings | | | | | | | |
| 3 or more siblings | -2.4 | -2.3 | -5.8 | | | -3.0 | -2.3 |
| Mother not HS graduate | | | | | | | |
| Mother some college | 1.9 | 1.8 | | | 3.4 | | |
| Mother college graduate | 7.3 | 7.4 | | | 12.7 | 12.6 | 6.3 |
| Father not HS graduate | | | | | | | |
| Father some college | 2.8 | 2.6 | 7.6 | | | | 3.2 |
| Father college graduate | 11.3 | 11.7 | 3.3 | 11.9 | 7.7 | 7.6 | 11.6 |
| Mother working | 1.8 | 1.8 | | | | | |

NOTE: Figures in this table were extracted from the final regression models as shown in Appendix B. A blank indicates that the variable was included in the model but was statistically insignificant.
[a]Conditional on having attended 10th grade.
[b]Conditional on having graduated from high school.

the influence of the mother to be greater than the influence of the father.

Youths whose *mothers worked* are less likely to graduate from high school than youths whose mothers did not; but once graduated from high school, youths with working mothers are more likely to go on to college and stay continuously through four years of college.

## Motivation and Parental Expectations

We used one measure—"likes working hard in school"—to assess the influence of motivation on educational attainment and two other measures—"mother wants respondent to go to college" and "parents always know where respondent is"—to assess the influence of parental expectations and support, respectively. All else equal, these three factors contributed more to our three educational attainment measures than any one of the other factors included in our models, underlining the importance of motivation to study and of family attitudes and support, neither of which can be easily influenced by educational institutions (Table 6.4).

*Liking to work hard in school* is generally positively associated with high school graduation, college-going, and continuity in college. But, there are differences in the size of the effect of this factor across racial/ethnic groups. The effect of "liking to work hard in school" is larger for Hispanics and whites than it is for Asians and blacks. In particular, blacks who like to work hard in school are no more likely to go to college than those who do not; however, the first are more likely to persevere once in college than the second.

*Youths whose mothers want them to go to college* do so at much higher rates and stay continuously longer than youths whose mothers do not. A mother's college expectation is also associated with high school graduation, but the positive effect is two to four times lower than it is for college-going. Also, the effect of a mother's college expectations is larger for immigrants than for natives, most particularly with respect to continuity in college. This effect on college-going is also larger for Hispanics and whites than it is for Asians and blacks. All else being equal, a Hispanic youth whose mother wants him/her to go to college is 25 percent more likely to go to college than a youth whose mother does not. However, the large effect of

## Table 6.4

**Motivational Factors Associated with Educational Attainment, for All and by Immigration Status and Race/Ethnicity**

| | All | Native | Immi-grant | Asian | Black | His-panic | White |
|---|---|---|---|---|---|---|---|
| **High School Graduates[a]** | | | | | | | |
| Works hard in school | 1.5 | 1.5 | | | | 3.3 | 1.7 |
| Mother wants youth to go to college | 4.7 | 4.6 | 7.9 | 6.2 | 4.4 | 4.0 | 4.8 |
| Parent always knows where youth is | 22.1 | 22.1 | 24.0 | 5.5 | 18.9 | 32.7 | 21.2 |
| **Went to Any College[b]** | | | | | | | |
| Works hard in school | 5.3 | 5.8 | −7.8 | | | 3.6 | 6.3 |
| Mother wants youth to go to college | 28.3 | 28.1 | 30.2 | 17.0 | 19.1 | 25.1 | 29.6 |
| Parent always knows where youth is | 4.7 | 4.6 | 8.8 | | 10.8 | 5.6 | 3.7 |
| **Was in College 42 Months or More[b]** | | | | | | | |
| Works hard in school | 5.7 | 5.7 | | 13.4 | 2.2 | 3.4 | 6.3 |
| Mother wants youth to go to college | 11.5 | 11.4 | 16.3 | 14.7 | 5.1 | 8.6 | 12.7 |
| Parent always knows where youth is | 3.9 | 3.5 | 13.8 | | 3.8 | | 4.4 |

NOTE: Figures in this table were extracted from the final regression models as shown in Appendix B. A blank indicates that the variable was included in the model but was statistically insignificant.

[a]Conditional on having attended 10th grade.

[b]Conditional on having graduated from high school.

Hispanic mothers' college expectations on their children is offset by the relatively low proportion of Hispanic mothers who hold this expectation (see Chapter Three).

*Youths whose parents know where they are at all times* are also much more likely to graduate from high school. This factor is also positively associated with college-going and continuity in college, but its effect is four to five times smaller than it is on high school graduation. There are no major differences in the magnitude of the effect of this factor between immigrants and natives and between racial/ethnic groups, with the exception of Asians. For the latter, the effect of this factor on high school graduation is three to five times smaller than for any other racial/ethnic group and it is not associated with college-going.

## Institutional Access

We noted above that because of data limitations, we did not have direct measures of institutional access for inclusion in this analysis. We had to settle for including regional, rural, and urban controls as proxies of institutional access (Table 6.5). Two tentative observations are worth making with respect to regional patterns.

First, immigrants are seemingly less likely to go to college in the Northeast and North Central regions than in the two other regions of the United States, whereas the reverse is true for natives.

### Table 6.5

### Regional, Rural, and City Factors Associated with Educational Attainment, for All and by Immigration Status and Race/Ethnicity

| | All | Native | Immigrant | Asian | Black | Hispanic | White |
|---|---|---|---|---|---|---|---|
| High School Graduates[a] | | | | | | | |
| Lives in Northeast | 2.6 | 2.7 | | | -3.5 | | 4.2 |
| Lives in North Central | 1.6 | 1.8 | -6.3 | | -7.6 | | 3.2 |
| Lives in West | -1.3 | -1.4 | | 6.1 | | | |
| Lives in rural area | | | 8.6 | | | 5.2 | -2.0 |
| Lives in large city | | | | | 3.4 | | |
| Went to Any College[b] | | | | | | | |
| Lives in Northeast | 2.1 | 2.5 | -7.5 | | 4.7 | | |
| Lives in North Central | 2.6 | 3.0 | -8.8 | | 8.7 | | |
| Lives in West | 5.1 | 5.2 | | | 15.0 | 12.6 | |
| Lives in rural area | -8.0 | -7.8 | -15.6 | -26.2 | | -11.0 | -7.9 |
| Lives in large city | 2.6 | | 10.3 | -3.9 | | 6.9 | |
| Was in College 42 Months or More[b] | | | | | | | |
| Lives in Northeast | 1.9 | 2.1 | | | | 2.6 | 2.4 |
| Lives in North Central | | | | | | | |
| Lives in West | -2.3 | -2.5 | | | | 3.9 | -3.3 |
| Lives in rural area | -4.8 | -4.9 | | | -3.6 | | -5.4 |
| Lives in large city | | | | | | | |

NOTE: Figures in this table were extracted from the final regression models as shown in Appendix B. A blank indicates that the variable was included in the model but was statistically insignificant.
[a]Conditional on having attended 10th grade.
[b]Conditional on having graduated from high school.

Second, youths in the Western region, which includes California, are less likely to graduate from high school than youths going to school in other regions. However, if they graduate from high school, they are more likely to attend college than their counterparts in other regions. And youths in the Western region are less likely to pursue college continuously. We have no explanation for these regional differences in "institutional access" and educational attainment. Further research should seek to confirm these differences and identify the reasons for them.

The rural versus urban differences are in the direction expected. Youths who are attending high school in a rural area are less likely to go on to college than youths from a nonrural high school. Attendance at a rural high school has a higher negative effect on immigrants than on natives. The reverse is true at the other end of the rural-urban spectrum. Immigrant youths who went to high school in a large city are more likely to go to college than natives—a finding that is consistent with the findings of Manski and Wise (1983).

## SUMMARY

This is the first study to systematically explore the relationship between immigrant secondary and postsecondary educational attainment and a number of individual and family characteristics and to compare these relationships with those found for natives. Our findings regarding participation in postsecondary education are summarized in Table 6.6. The findings for graduation from high school are not included in this table, but they mirror these findings.

Immigration status was *not* found to be independently associated with college-going, but it was positively and independently associated with attending college continuously for four years immediately following high school graduation.

The individual and family factors associated with college attendance were found to be generally similar for both immigrants and natives. Parental education, most particularly that of the father, *and* parental expectations for, and support of, the children's education are both

## Table 6.6

### Summary of Factors Associated with Postsecondary Education, Natives and Immigrants

| Independent Variables | All | | Native | | Immigrant | |
|---|---|---|---|---|---|---|
| | Any College | 42 Months or more | Any College | 42 Months or more | Any College | 42 Months or more |
| **Individual Characteristics** | | | | | | |
| Immigration status | | + | NR | NR | − | − |
| ≤ 5 years in U.S. | | | NR | NR | | |
| 6–10 years in U.S. | − | − | NR | NR | | |
| Asian | | + | | + | + | |
| Black | − | − | | − | | |
| Hispanic | − | − | − | − | | |
| White | | | | | | |
| Female | + | − | + | | | − |
| English proficiency | − | | | − | | |
| **Family Characteristics** | | | | | | |
| Income < $16K | − | − | − | − | | − |
| Income >$25K | + | + | + | + | | |
| No siblings | | | − | | | |
| 3 or more siblings | − | − | − | − | − | − |
| Mother not high school graduate | − | | − | | | |
| Mother some college | + | + | + | + | | |
| Mother college grad. | + | + | + | + | | |
| Father not high school graduate | − | | − | | | |
| Father some college | + | + | + | + | + | + |
| Father college grad. | + | + | + | + | + | + |
| Mother working | + | + | + | + | + | |
| **Motivation and Expectations** | | | | | | |
| Works hard in school | + | + | + | + | − | |
| Mother wants youth to go to college | + | + | + | + | + | + |
| Parent always knows where youth is | + | + | + | + | + | + |
| **Institutional Access** | | | | | | |
| Lives in Northeast | + | + | + | + | − | |
| Lives in North Central | + | | + | | − | |
| Lives in West | + | − | + | − | | |
| Lives in rural area | − | − | − | − | − | |
| Lives in large city | + | | | | + | |

NOTE: See Appendix A for definition of variables. NR means variable is not relevant to this model.

strongly and independently associated with eventual pursuit of a postsecondary education upon high school graduation. This confirms the importance of family background and family attitudes toward education in determining the eventual educational attainment of both immigrant and native children. Their college-going is also affected by two other family characteristics. It is positively associated with the mother working, confirming the positive "demonstration" effect of mothers in the work force. And it is negatively associated with having three or more siblings in the family, supporting the notion that finite parental resources are spread ever thinner as there are more children in the family.

With the exception of Asian immigrants, who were found to be independently associated with higher rates of college-going, race/ ethnicity was *not* found to be associated with participation in postsecondary education for immigrants including Hispanics and blacks. In contrast, race/ethnicity was strongly and negatively associated with some college-going natives, most especially Hispanic natives.

Because we found greater differences across racial/ethnic groups than between immigrants and natives in high school graduation rates (Chapter Four) and rates of participation in postsecondary education (Chapter Five), we also explored the relationship between educational attainment and immigration status, individual and family factors for each racial/ethnic group separately. Our findings regarding participation in postsecondary education are summarized in Table 6.7. Findings for high school graduation are not included in this table but they also mirror these findings.

There are more commonalities than differences across racial/ethnic groups in the factors associated with college-going. Fathers' education *and* parental expectations regarding their children's eventual education attainment were found to be strongly and independently associated with postsecondary education for all racial/ethnic groups, again underlining the importance of parental educational background and expectations for their children. Students' attitudes toward working hard in school were also associated with increased participation in postsecondary education regardless of race or ethnicity, particularly with respect to pursuing four continuous years of college.

## Table 6.7

### Summary of Factors Associated with Postsecondary Education, by Race/Ethnicity

| Independent Variables | Any College | | | | 42 Months or More | | | |
|---|---|---|---|---|---|---|---|---|
| | Asian | Black | His-panic | White | Asian | Black | His-panic | White |
| **Individual Characteristics** | | | | | | | | |
| Immigrant | | + | + | | + | + | | |
| ≤ 5 years in U.S. | | − | | | | | − | |
| 6–10 years in U.S. | − | | | | | | − | |
| Female | | | | | | | − | |
| English proficiency | − | | − | | | | | |
| **Family Characteristics** | | | | | | | | |
| Income < $16K | | − | − | − | − | | | − |
| Income >$25K | | + | + | | | | + | + |
| No siblings | | − | | | | | | |
| 3 or more siblings | | − | − | | | − | | − |
| Mother not high school graduate | | − | − | | | | | |
| Mother some college | | + | + | + | + | | | |
| Mother college grad. | | + | + | + | + | | + | + |
| Father not high school graduate | | | | − | | | | |
| Father some college | | + | + | + | | | | + |
| Father college grad. | + | + | + | + | + | + | + | + |
| Mother working | | + | + | | | | | |
| **Motivation and Expectations** | | | | | | | | |
| Works hard in school | | | + | + | + | + | + | + |
| Mother wants youth to go to college | + | + | + | + | + | + | + | + |
| Parent always knows where youth is | | + | + | + | + | | | + |
| **Institutional Access** | | | | | | | | |
| Lives in Northeast | | + | | | | | + | + |
| Lives in North Central | | + | | | | | | |
| Lives in West | | + | + | | | | + | − |
| Lives in rural area | | − | − | | − | | | − |
| Lives in large city | | + | | | | | | |

NOTE:  See Appendix A for definition of variables.

Also, low incomes and having three or more siblings were negatively associated with postsecondary education for all racial/ethnic groups.[8]

A few notable factors were found to be specific to only one or two racial/ethnic groups. Immigration status led to higher participation in postsecondary education for black and Hispanic immigrants, but not for whites and Asians. This finding combined with the finding that Hispanic origin has a strong and independent negative effect on educational attainment raises the question of why Hispanics may behave differently from other racial/ethnic groups. Further research needs to address this basic question if ways are to be found to increase the educational achievements of Hispanics. Given the sizable lag in their educational attainment and the growing size of the Hispanic population in the nation, this is rapidly becoming an urgent issue.

Gender was found not to be associated with college-going for all ethnic groups, with the exception of Hispanics. Hispanic females were significantly less likely to pursue four years of college than their male counterparts.

---

[8]Although this factor is not significant in the estimates for Asians, we suspect that this is due to the relatively smaller number of Asians in the HSB database

# Chapter Seven

# CONCLUSIONS AND POLICY IMPLICATIONS

The number of immigrant children and youths in American schools, colleges, and universities has increased rapidly over the past 20 years and is expected to continue to increase in years to come. Combined with the children of immigrants born in the United States, they are rapidly changing the racial/ethnic composition of the student body, most particularly in those states where immigrants concentrate, such as California, New York, and Florida. Already today, the majority of students in California's high schools are of Hispanic and Asian origin.

These rapid changes in the composition of the student body have raised questions about the ability of educational institutions to respond effectively to the unique needs of these "new" populations, and in turn about the educational performance of immigrants in American institutions. This concern stems from the fact that immigrant children and the children of immigrants provide a growing share of new entries in the labor force and hence are of increasing importance to the nation's economic future.

This study is the first to systematically focus on the attainment of immigrant children and youths in American schools. Our main findings and their policy implications are summarized below:

1. *Immigrant students and their parents hold more positive attitudes toward schooling and have higher expectations for a college education than native students and their parents.*

Immigrant children and parents of all racial/ethnic groups studied have higher educational aspirations than their native counterparts.

However, the difference in aspirations is three times greater between immigrants and natives of Hispanic origin than it is between immigrants and natives of other groups. Where educational aspirations and working hard to fulfill them are concerned, Hispanic immigrants are generally similar to immigrants of other racial/ethnic origins. These relative aspirations, however, are not maintained among Hispanic natives and their parents, who have the lowest ratings on indicators of college aspirations. These findings, based on a national sample, are similar to recent findings based on a study of children in San Diego schools (Suárez-Orozco and Suárez-Orozco, 1995).

Because we found a significant relationship between attitudes and aspirations toward education of both students and parents on eventual educational attainment, the reasons for this significant decline of educational aspirations encountered among Hispanic youths and their parents should be thoroughly researched.

2. *All else equal, the higher educational aspirations of immigrants translate into higher rates of college-going for them than for natives.*

Whatever difficulties immigrant children and youths might face adjusting to the language and institutional and cultural norms of this country, their educational attainment equals or exceeds that of native children and youths. We found that holding income, education of parents, and other individual and family factors constant, immigrants were more likely to go to college, not so much because they are immigrants, per se, but because they hold higher educational aspirations. In U.S. high schools, immigrants were also more likely to have been placed on an academic track, to have taken advanced courses in math and sciences, and to have taken the ACT or SAT tests.

Although these findings do not support the need to develop policies targeted uniquely on immigrants, they do mean that the increasing number of immigrants in U.S. schools raises new and unique demands for U.S. educational institutions. Two companion RAND studies—one focusing on responses of primary and secondary schools (McDonnell and Hill, 1993) and the other on responses of postsecondary educational institutions to immigration (Gray and Rolph, 1996)—have documented the current difficulties that schools and colleges are having meeting the special language and social sup-

port needs of immigrants and how they are straining their adminis-
trative functions and operations.  In postsecondary institutions, the
growing presence of immigrants also raises fundamental questions
regarding graduating requirements (most particularly with respect to
proficiency in the English language), equity in the allocation of financial assistance between immigrants and natives, and the definition of "disadvantaged and underrepresented" students in the face of
increased diversity.  Furthermore, immigration has given rise to new
issues that public policy needs to address, as we identify below.

3. *The largest discrepancies in educational attainment are to be found
between racial/ethnic groups regardless of immigration status.  It is
these discrepancies that will present the greatest public policy chal-
lenge in years to come.*

It is well documented that the educational attainment of Asians and
whites is higher than that of blacks and Hispanics.  What this study
shows is that the same large differences in educational attainment
are to be found among immigrants from different racial/ethnic
groups.  Hispanic immigrants scored the lowest of any racial/ethnic
group on nearly all indicators of course-taking, educational expectations, and college-going considered in this study, just as their native
counterparts of Hispanic origin do.  At the same time, just as immigrant and native Hispanics' college preparation and college-going
rates are consistently the lowest, those of Asians are consistently the
highest, with whites and blacks in between.

Continuation of these discrepancies in educational attainment is
cause for concern for two reasons.  First, Hispanics constitute a
growing share of the nation's students—a growth that has been
fueled by 20 years of continuous and expanding immigration from
Mexico and Central America.[1]  Today, one in ten high school students nationwide is of Hispanic origin, about the same proportion as
the African American population in high school.  That proportion is
much higher in some states.  In California, one out of every three
high school students is of Hispanic origin, and it is expected that at
least two out of every five students will be of Hispanic origin by year

---

[1]Because Hispanics are younger and have higher fertility rates than other racial/ethnic
groups, their relative growth will continue regardless of whether Congress approves
legislation that would reduce the level of immigration to that of the 1980s.

2005 within cohorts of students that are expected to be 20 to 25 percent larger than those of today. The level of education that these students achieve will in large part determine the future quality of the labor force.

A second reason is that educational institutions *alone* cannot enhance significantly the educational attainment of Hispanics (and other similarly situated youths). We found that, by and large, the same individual and family factors significantly affect the high school graduation and college-going rates of all racial/ethnic groups and of natives and immigrants. These factors include family resources, education of parents, and attitudes toward and expectations for education of both students and their parents. It is the difference between Hispanics and other racial/ethnic groups in the value of these factors that in most part explains why Hispanics' educational attainment is lower than that of other groups.[2] We have shown in Chapter Two that Hispanics are at least twice as likely to have an income in the lowest quartile and more than three times more likely to have two parents with less than a high school education. And Hispanic students and their parents have lower educational aspirations than members of other ethnic groups.

Income assistance and financial assistance for education can alleviate the income gap between Hispanics and other groups. But funding for these programs is being reduced at the same time as college tuition and fees have been increasing very rapidly. Short of a reversal of current budgetary and policy trends, low income will remain a barrier to the enhancement of educational attainment of not only low-income Hispanics but of all students in low-income families.

The other two factors—low education levels of parents and educational expectations of students and of parents for their children—may not be easily amenable to change. Certainly, programs directed at increasing parental involvement in the education of their children and adult education programs including English language instruction, high school equivalency classes, vocational training, and work-

---

[2]We do not argue that the individual and family factors considered in this study are the only ones determining educational attainment, only that these factors play a significant role.

shops on effective parenting are steps in the right direction. But demand for these programs far exceeds the supply, and funding for such programs has been declining at the same time as the need for them has been growing. Furthermore, we do not know how effective these relatively new programs are with respect to enhancing the educational attainment of targeted youths. A few English and literacy classes are unlikely to compensate for an education that for many Hispanic immigrant parents stopped at the 8th grade or even below. And we do not fully understand the considerations and processes that affect students' educational expectations and those of parents for their children and why these expectations have been found to decline across generations of immigrants. Further research is needed to develop strategies that specifically address these barriers to increased educational attainment.

*4. Immigrant youths, most particularly those of Hispanic origin, who enter the country after the age of 15 or so, are less likely to enter the U.S. school system or stay in school than children who come at an earlier age. The number of such children is not negligible.*

In-school participation rates of high school age youths are generally similar to those for Asian, black, and white natives, hovering around 91 to 95 percent. In contrast, only 73 percent of immigrant youths of Mexican origin and 88 percent of other Hispanics (mostly Central American) are reported to be in school. We provided some evidence (Chapter Two) that these youths are not just drop-outs from U.S. schools; rather, they are failing to "drop in" to the school system in the first place. In any one year, the number of such immigrant youths has not been very large—about 37,000 and 25,000 nationwide and in California, respectively, or about 4 and 2 percent of the high-school-age cohort, respectively. Over time, however, the number of these youths is growing rapidly, reaching hundreds of thousands of young adults without a high school diploma and, hence, with low prospects for economic mobility over their lifetime.

Strategies to encourage these youths to continue their education in the United States need to be developed. School-based outreach programs may be helpful in this respect, although they will probably not be sufficient. These youths are likely to have been out of school for a year or more in their country of origin even before arriving here. They may also have to work to support themselves and their families.

Thus, they may not have the capabilities to pursue an education in U.S. schools without receiving considerable remedial education, and they may face strong financial disincentives to do so in the first place.

In conclusion, today's immigrants may be performing in U.S. educational institutions as well if not better than their native counterparts. But the racial/ethnic compositional change that has been driven by immigration over the past 25 years has created a situation in which a growing segment of the population, primarily of Hispanic origin, significantly lags other racial/ethnic groups in its educational attainment.  In some areas of the country, the proportion of such youths exceeds one-third, jeopardizing not only their own future economic opportunities but also the quality of tomorrow's labor force.  It is also increasing the demand placed on public services. Enhancing the educational attainment of these children and youths is not a task that the country's educational institutions can accomplish alone.  Effective strategies directed at overcoming parental low income, low education, and low educational expectations for their children must also be designed and implemented.

# DEFINITIONS, MEANS, AND STANDARD ERRORS
# OF VARIABLES

This appendix presents the definitions, the means, and the standard errors of both dependent and independent variables (Tables A.1 through A.3).

### Table A.1

### Definition of Variables

| Variable Name | Definition |
|---|---|
| | Dependent Variables |
| High school graduation | = 1, if has high school diploma by 4th year after high school senior year<br>= 0, otherwise |
| Any college | = 1, if attended a 2-year and/or 4-year college at any time during the 4 years after high school senior year<br>= 0, otherwise |
| 42 months of college | = 1, if attended college for 42 months or more during the 4 years after high school senior year<br>= 0, otherwise |

## Table A.1 (continued)

| Independent Variables | |
| --- | --- |
| **Individual Characteristics** | |
| Immigrant | = 1, if born outside the United States |
| | = 0, otherwise |
| Length of Stay in U.S. | |
| ≤ 5 years | = 1, if has been in U.S. 5 years or less |
| | = 0, otherwise |
| 6–10 years | = 1, if has been in U.S. 6–10 years |
| | = 0, otherwise |
| Race, Ethnicity | |
| Asian | = 1, if youth is of Asian origin |
| | = 0, otherwise |
| Black | = 1, if youth is black |
| | = 0, otherwise |
| Hispanic | = 1, if youth is of Hispanic origin |
| | = 0, otherwise |
| Female | = 1, if youth is female |
| | = 0, otherwise |
| English proficiency | = 1, if youth lives in household where dominant language is English |
| | = 0, otherwise |
| **Family Characteristics** | |
| Income <$16,000 | = 1, if family income is $16,000 or less |
| | = 0, otherwise |
| Income > $25,000 | = 1, if family income is $25,000 or more |
| | = 0, otherwise |
| Size | |
| No siblings | = 1, if has no siblings |
| | = 0, otherwise |
| 3 or more siblings | = 1, if has 3 or more brothers or sisters |
| | = 0, otherwise |
| Mother's Education | |
| Less than high school | = 1, if highest education level is less than high school |
| | = 0, otherwise |
| Some college | = 1, if highest education level is "attended college" but has no degree |
| | = 0, otherwise |
| College graduate | = 1, if highest education level is "finished college" or higher |
| | = 0, otherwise |
| Father's Education | |
| Less than high school | = 1, if highest education level is less than high school |
| | = 0, otherwise |
| Some college | = 1, if highest education level is "attended college" but has no degree |
| | = 0, otherwise |

## Table A.1 (continued)

| | |
|---|---|
| College graduate | = 1, if highest education level is "finished college" or higher |
| | = 0, otherwise |
| Mother working | = 1, if mother ever worked |
| | = 0, otherwise |

Motivation and Expectations

| | |
|---|---|
| Works hard in school | = 1, if likes to work hard in school |
| | = 0, otherwise |
| Parental expectations | = 1, if mother wants youth to go to college |
| | = 0, otherwise |
| Parental oversight | = 1, if parents always know where respondent is |
| | = 0, otherwise |

Institutional Access
Region dummies

| | |
|---|---|
| Northeast | = 1, if youth's high school is in Northeast region |
| | = 0, otherwise |
| North Central | = 1, if youth's high school is in North Central region |
| | = 0, otherwise |
| West | = 1, if youth's high school is in Western region |
| | = 0, otherwise |
| Rural area | = 1, if youth's high school location is rural |
| | = 0, otherwise |
| Large city location | = 1, if youth's high school is in city or suburb of 500,000 |
| | = 0, otherwise |

## Table A.2

## Means and Standard Errors for Dependent Variables

| | All | | Native | | Immi-grant | | Asian | | Black | | His-panic | | White | |
|---|---|---|---|---|---|---|---|---|---|---|---|---|---|---|
| | M | SE | M | SE | M | SE | M | SE | M | SE | M | SE | M | SE |
| High school graduate | .90 | .30 | .90 | .31 | .89 | .23 | .95 | .14 | .87 | .27 | .83 | .27 | .91 | .33 |
| Any college | .60 | .49 | .60 | .50 | .68 | .34 | .81 | .25 | .55 | .39 | .47 | .35 | .63 | .56 |
| 42 months of college | .16 | .37 | .16 | .38 | .22 | .30 | .31 | .30 | .11 | .24 | .09 | .20 | .18 | .45 |

Table A.3

Means and Standard Errors for Independent Variables

| | All | | Native | | Immigrant | | Asian | | Black | | Hispanic | | White | |
|---|---|---|---|---|---|---|---|---|---|---|---|---|---|---|
| | M | SE | M | SE | M | SE | M | SE | M | SE | M | SE | M | SE |
| **Individual Characteristics** | | | | | | | | | | | | | | |
| Immigrant | .04 | .19 | | | | | .50 | .32 | .04 | .15 | .11 | .22 | .02 | .17 |
| ≤5 years in U.S. | .01 | .09 | | | .18 | .29 | .24 | .28 | .01 | .07 | .02 | .11 | .00 | .06 |
| 6–10 years in U.S. | .01 | .12 | | | .21 | .30 | .11 | .20 | .02 | .10 | .04 | .15 | .01 | .10 |
| English proficiency | .96 | .19 | .98 | .16 | .63 | .36 | .63 | .31 | 1.0 | .05 | .78 | .29 | .99 | .11 |
| Asian | .01 | .11 | .01 | .08 | .16 | .27 | | | | | | | | |
| Black | .11 | .32 | .11 | .32 | .11 | .23 | | | | | | | | |
| Hispanic | .12 | .32 | .11 | .32 | .32 | .35 | | | | | | | | |
| Female | .51 | .50 | .51 | .51 | .49 | .37 | .49 | .32 | .54 | .40 | .47 | .36 | .51 | .58 |
| **Family Characteristics** | | | | | | | | | | | | | | |
| Income < $16K | .31 | .46 | .31 | .47 | .33 | .35 | .33 | .30 | .47 | .40 | .44 | .36 | .27 | .51 |
| Income > $25K | .23 | .42 | .23 | .43 | .19 | .29 | .26 | .28 | .11 | .25 | .14 | .25 | .26 | .51 |
| No siblings | .11 | .32 | .11 | .32 | .11 | .23 | .07 | .16 | .21 | .33 | .16 | .26 | .10 | .34 |
| 3 or more siblings | .47 | .50 | .47 | .51 | .46 | .37 | .49 | .32 | .55 | .40 | .54 | .36 | .45 | .58 |
| Mother not high school graduate | .18 | .38 | .17 | .38 | .25 | .32 | .19 | .25 | .22 | .33 | .33 | .34 | .15 | .41 |
| Mother some college | .22 | .41 | .21 | .42 | .23 | .31 | .24 | .28 | .20 | .32 | .15 | .26 | .23 | .49 |
| Mother college grad. | .12 | .33 | .12 | .34 | .11 | .23 | .19 | .26 | .08 | .22 | .06 | .17 | .14 | .40 |
| Father not high school graduate | .20 | .40 | .20 | .41 | .24 | .31 | .13 | .22 | .24 | .34 | .33 | .34 | .18 | .44 |
| Father some college | .19 | .39 | .19 | .40 | .16 | .27 | .22 | .27 | .13 | .27 | .15 | .26 | .21 | .47 |
| Father college grad. | .19 | .39 | .18 | .39 | .22 | .31 | .31 | .30 | .07 | .21 | .09 | .20 | .22 | .48 |
| Mother working | .85 | .35 | .86 | .36 | .81 | .29 | .84 | .24 | .79 | .33 | .80 | .29 | .87 | .39 |

## Table A.3 (continued)

| | All | | Native | | Immigrant | | Asian | | Black | | Hispanic | | White | |
|---|---|---|---|---|---|---|---|---|---|---|---|---|---|---|
| | M | SE | M | SE | M | SE | M | SE | M | SE | M | SE | M | SE |
| Motivation | | | | | | | | | | | | | | |
| Works hard in school | .50 | .50 | .50 | .51 | .60 | .36 | .63 | .31 | .60 | .39 | .51 | .36 | .48 | .58 |
| Mother wants youth to go to college | .56 | .50 | .56 | .51 | .65 | .35 | .77 | .27 | .56 | .40 | .46 | .36 | .57 | .57 |
| Parent always knows where youth is | .68 | .47 | .68 | .47 | .69 | .34 | .70 | .30 | .61 | .39 | .63 | .35 | .70 | .53 |
| Institutional Access | | | | | | | | | | | | | | |
| Lives in Northeast | .22 | .41 | .22 | .42 | .24 | .32 | .12 | .21 | .18 | .31 | .15 | .25 | .24 | .49 |
| Lives in North Central | .29 | .45 | .29 | .46 | .18 | .28 | .12 | .21 | .18 | .31 | .17 | .27 | .33 | .54 |
| Lives in West | .16 | .37 | .16 | .37 | .28 | .33 | .61 | .31 | .06 | .19 | .25 | .31 | .16 | .42 |
| Lives in rural area | .16 | .37 | .16 | .38 | .03 | .16 | .03 | .10 | .10 | .24 | .16 | .26 | .17 | .44 |
| Lives in large city | .11 | .31 | .10 | .31 | .21 | .30 | .21 | .26 | .16 | .30 | .14 | .25 | .09 | .33 |

# REGRESSION RESULTS

The three tables in this appendix show the linear (OLS) results for each educational outcome measure. Each table includes a column for each of the seven samples analyzed (all youths, natives, immigrants, Asians, blacks, Hispanics, and whites). Specific definitions for dependent and independent variables are shown in Appendix A, Table A.1.

## Table B.1

## OLS Regression Results for High School Graduation

| | All | Native | Immi-grant | Asian | Black | His-panic | White |
|---|---|---|---|---|---|---|---|
| **Individual Characteristics** | | | | | | | |
| Immigrant | .001 | | | .051$^+$ | −.047 | .012 | .005 |
| ≤ 5 years in U.S. | .005 | | .005 | .006 | .139$^+$ | −.019 | −.038 |
| 6–10 years in U.S. | −.012 | | .001 | .025 | .080 | −.084$^{++}$ | .001 |
| Asian | .045$^+$ | .019 | .030 | | | | |
| Black | −.003 | −.002 | −.031 | | | | |
| Hispanic | −.029$^{+++}$ | −.024$^{+++}$ | −.089$^{+++}$ | | | | |
| Female | −.008$^+$ | −.008$^+$ | .002 | .014 | .023$^+$ | −.015 | −.011$^+$ |
| English proficiency | .031$^{++}$ | −.038$^{++}$ | .013 | .028 | .041 | .050$^{+++}$ | −.027 |
| **Family Characteristics** | | | | | | | |
| Income < $16K | −.009$^+$ | −.008 | −.0323 | −.004 | .007 | −.054$^{+++}$ | −.004 |
| Income > $25K | .016$^{++}$ | .017$^{+++}$ | .011 | .000 | .037$^+$ | .035$^+$ | .013$^+$ |
| No siblings | −.041$^{+++}$ | −.043$^{+++}$ | −.006 | −.025 | −.058$^{+++}$ | −.017 | −.038$^{+++}$ |
| 3 or more siblings | −.017$^{+++}$ | −.018$^{+++}$ | −.003 | .014 | −.0253 | −.016 | −.019$^{+++}$ |
| Mother not high school graduate | −.055$^{+++}$ | −.057$^{+++}$ | −.029 | .075$^{++}$ | −.042$^+$ | −.037$^{++}$ | −.064$^{+++}$ |
| Mother some college | .004 | .005 | −.022 | .099$^{+++}$ | .019 | .000 | .002 |
| Mother college grad. | .016$^+$ | .017$^+$ | .005 | .053 | .030 | .036 | .014 |
| Father not high school graduate | −.014$^{++}$ | −.015$^{++}$ | .0 | −.062$^+$ | .003 | −.015 | −.018$^{++}$ |
| Father some college | .016$^{++}$ | .016$^{++}$ | −.029 | −.067$^{++}$ | .021 | .020 | .015$^+$ |
| Father college grad. | .024$^{+++}$ | .022$^{+++}$ | .064$^{++}$ | −.021 | .000 | .057$^+$ | .021$^{++}$ |
| Mother working | −.034$^{+++}$ | −.033$^{+++}$ | −.065$^{+++}$ | .007 | −.0253 | −.049$^{+++}$ | −.037$^{+++}$ |
| **Motivation and Expectations** | | | | | | | |
| Works hard in school | .015$^{+++}$ | .015$^{+++}$ | .021 | .021 | −.017 | .033$^{+++}$ | .017$^{+++}$ |
| Mother wants youth to go to college | .047$^{+++}$ | .046$^{+++}$ | .079$^{+++}$ | .062$^{++}$ | .044$^{+++}$ | .040$^{+++}$ | .048$^{+++}$ |
| Parent always knows where youth is | .221$^{+++}$ | .221$^{+++}$ | .240$^{+++}$ | .055$^{++}$ | .189$^{+++}$ | .327$^{+++}$ | .212$^{+++}$ |
| **Institutional Access** | | | | | | | |
| Lives in Northeast | .026$^{+++}$ | .027$^{+++}$ | .015 | .034 | −.035$^+$ | .007 | .042$^{+++}$ |
| Lives in North Central | .016$^{++}$ | .018$^{+++}$ | −.063$^{++}$ | .020 | −.076$^{+++}$ | .003 | .032$^{+++}$ |
| Lives in West | −.013$^+$ | −.014$^+$ | .007 | .061$^+$ | −.002 | −.004 | −.009 |
| Lives in rural area | −.007 | −.009 | .086$^{++}$ | −.010 | .015 | .052$^{+++}$ | −.020$^+$ |
| Lives in large city | −.005 | −.005 | .000 | .024 | −.034$^+$ | −.011 | .007 |
| $R^2$ | .17 | .17 | .22 | .12 | .11 | .22 | .18 |

NOTE: $^+$ = p < 0.05; $^{++}$ p = < 0.01; $^{+++}$ = p < 0.001; otherwise coefficient is not significant.

## Table B.2

## OLS Regression Results for Any College

| | All | Native | Immi-grants | Asian | Black | His-panic | White |
|---|---|---|---|---|---|---|---|
| **Individual Characteristics** | | | | | | | |
| Immigrant | .029 | | | .005 | .113+ | .105+++ | −.016 |
| ≤ 5 years in U.S. | −.007 | | .028 | .035 | −.136 | −.148++ | .114 |
| 6–10 years in U.S. | −.064+ | | −.022 | −.030 | −.253+++ | −.049 | −.036 |
| Asian | .050 | .039 | .122++ | | | | |
| Black | −.005 | −.004 | −.007 | | | | |
| Hispanic | −.074+++ | −.082+++ | .032 | | | | |
| Female | .015++ | .016+ | −.008 | .002 | .028 | .021 | .012 |
| English proficiency | −.092+++ | −.110+++ | .019 | −.081+ | .111 | −.093+++ | −.040 |
| **Family Characteristics** | | | | | | | |
| Income < $16K | −.019++ | −.020+ | .003 | −.008 | .037+ | −.053+++ | −.024+ |
| Income > $25K | .033+++ | .035+++ | .013 | .059 | .049 | .041+ | .028++ |
| No siblings | −.017 | −.016 | −.036 | −.015 | −.058+ | −.002 | −.011 |
| 3 or more siblings | −.034+++ | −.034+++ | −.072++ | −.041 | .041+ | −.016 | −.035+++ |
| Mother not high school graduate | −.054+++ | −.059+++ | .012 | .025 | −.028 | −.042+ | −.068+++ |
| Mother some college | .070+++ | .074+++ | −.033 | .057 | .123+++ | .071+++ | .064+++ |
| Mother college grad. | .102+++ | .107+++ | −.037 | −.001 | .131+++ | .148+++ | .096+++ |
| Father not high school graduate | −.044+++ | −.042+++ | −.047 | .016 | .017 | .006 | −.067+++ |
| Father some college | .082+++ | .081+++ | .122+++ | .065 | .103+++ | .043+ | .081+++ |
| Father college grad. | .160+++ | .160+++ | .135+++ | .119++ | .079+ | .187+++ | .158+++ |
| Mother working | .031++ | .030++ | .061+ | .051 | .057++ | .068+++ | .019 |
| **Motivation and Expectations** | | | | | | | |
| Works hard in school | .053+++ | .058+++ | −.078++ | .043 | .005 | .036+ | .063+++ |
| Mother wants youth to go to college | .283+++ | .281+++ | .302+++ | .170+++ | .191+++ | .251+++ | .296+++ |
| Parent always knows where youth is | .047+++ | .046+++ | .088++ | −.005 | .108+++ | .056+++ | .037+++ |
| **Institutional Access** | | | | | | | |
| Lives in Northeast | .021++ | .025++ | −.075+ | −.041 | .047+ | .002 | .019 |
| Lives in North Central | .026+++ | .030+++ | −.088+ | −.056 | .087+++ | .024 | .018 |
| Lives in West | .051+++ | .052+++ | −.012 | −.011 | .150+++ | .126+++ | .026 |
| Lives in rural area | −.080+++ | −.078+++ | −.156++ | −.262++ | .004 | −.110+++ | −.079+++ |
| Lives in large city | .026++ | .019 | .103+++ | −.039 | .011 | .069+++ | .025 |
| $R^2$ | .23 | .23 | .21 | .12 | .13 | .21 | .24 |

NOTE: + = p < 0.05; ++ p = < 0.01; +++ = p < 0.001; otherwise coefficient is not significant.

## Table B.3

## OLS Regression Results for 42 Months of College

| | All | Native | Immi-grants | Asian | Black | His-panic | White |
|---|---|---|---|---|---|---|---|
| Individual Characteristics | | | | | | | |
| Immigrant | .048++ | | | −.015 | .075+ | .108+ | .032 |
| ≤ 5 years in U.S. | −.051 | | −.018 | −.051 | .039 | −.100+ | −.073 |
| 6–10 years in U.S. | −.074++ | | −.036 | −.152+ | −.078 | −.085+ | −.061 |
| Asian | .086+++ | .117+++ | .059 | | | | |
| Black | −.033+++ | −.035+++ | .021 | | | | |
| Hispanic | −.035+++ | −.037+++ | −.018 | | | | |
| Female | −.013++ | −.010 | −.100+++ | .012 | −.016 | −.017+ | −.013 |
| English proficiency | −.015 | −.005 | −.027 | −.058 | .106 | −.002 | −.018 |
| Family Characteristics | | | | | | | |
| Income < $16K | −.015++ | −.013+ | −.060+ | .024 | −.009++ | −.006 | −.019+ |
| Income > $25K | .044+++ | .047+++ | −.040 | .075 | .020 | .036++ | .045+++ |
| No siblings | −.014 | −.012 | −.066++ | .074 | −.049 | −.015 | −.008 |
| 3 or more siblings | −.024+++ | −.023+++ | −.058 | −.051 | −.020 | −.030++ | −.023++ |
| Mother not high school graduate | −.013 | −.015 | −.009 | .017 | −.013 | −.007 | −.015 |
| Mother some college | .019++ | .018++ | .038 | .055 | .034+ | .006 | .017 |
| Mother college grad. | .073+++ | .074+++ | .054 | .109 | .127+++ | .126+++ | .063+++ |
| Father not high school graduate | −.012 | −.012 | −.009 | .038 | −.005 | .007 | −.018 |
| Father some college | .028+++ | .026+++ | .076+ | −.020 | .003 | .015 | .032++ |
| Father college grad. | .113+++ | .117+++ | .033 | .119+ | .077+++ | .076+++ | .116+++ |
| Mother working | .018++ | .018+ | .034 | .004 | .024 | .019 | .016 |
| Motivation and Expectations | | | | | | | |
| Works hard in school | .057+++ | .057+++ | .034 | .134+++ | .022+ | .034+++ | .063+++ |
| Mother wants youth to go to college | .115+++ | .114+++ | .163+++ | .147++ | .051+++ | .086+++ | .127+++ |
| Parent always knows where youth is | .039+++ | .035+++ | .138+++ | −.003 | .038+++ | .014 | .044+++ |
| Institutional Access | | | | | | | |
| Lives in Northeast | .019++ | .021++ | −.018 | −.005 | −.013 | .026+ | .024+ |
| Lives in North Central | .007 | .007 | .024 | −.062 | −.009 | .009 | .010 |
| Lives in West | −.023++ | −.025++ | −.017 | .006 | −.036 | .039+++ | −.033++ |
| Lives in rural area | −.048+++ | −.049+++ | .056 | −.052 | −.036+ | −.009 | −.054+++ |
| Lives in large city | .010 | .008 | .036 | .083 | −.011 | .010 | .016 |
| $R^2$ | .12 | .12 | .12 | .12 | .06 | .10 | .12 |

NOTE: $^+$ = $p < 0.05$; $^{++}$ p = < 0.01; $^{+++}$ = $p < 0.001$; otherwise coefficient is not significant.

# REFERENCES

Benjamin, R., et al., *The Redesign of Governance in Higher Education*, Santa Monica, Calif.: RAND, MR-222-LE, 1993.

Blake, J., *Family Size and Achievement*, Berkeley, Calif.: University of California Press, 1989.

Borjas, G. J., "The Economics of Immigration," *Journal of Economic Literature*, Vol. XXXII, No. 4, 1994, pp. 1667–1717.

Borjas, G. J., *Friends or Strangers*, New York: Basic Books, Inc., 1990.

Bradley, R. H., "The Home Inventory: Rationale and Research," in J. Lachenmeyer and M. Gibbs (eds.), *Recent Research in Develop mental Psychopathology*, Gardner, N.Y.: Book Supplement to the *Journal of Child Psychology and Psychiatry*, 1985, pp. 191–201.

Caplan, N., J. K. Whitmore, and M. H. Choy, *The Boat People and Achievement in America: A Study of Family Life, Hard Work, and Cultural Values*, Ann Arbor, Mich.: University of Michigan Press, 1989.

Chiswick, B., "The Economic Progress of Immigrants: Some Apparently Universal Patterns," in William Fellner (ed.), *Contemporary Economic Problems 1979*, Washington, D.C.: American Enterprise Institute, 1979, pp. 357–399.

Carnoy, Martin, Hugh M. Daley, and Raul Hinojosa Ojeda, "The Changing Economic Position of Latinos in the U.S. Labor Market Since 1939," in Rebecca Morales and Frank Bonilla (eds.),

*Latinos in a Changing u.S. Economy*, Newbury Park, Calif.: Sage Publications, 1993, pp. 28–54.

Duran, B. J., and R. E. Weffer, "Immigrant's Aspirations, High School Process, and Academic Outcomes," *American Educational Research Journal*, Vol. 29, No. 1, 1992, pp. 163–181.

Fernandez, M. S., "Issues in Counseling Southeast-Asian Students," *Journal of Multicultural Counseling and Development*, Vol. 16, 1988, pp. 157–166.

Fernandez-Barillas, H. J., and T. L. Morrison, "Cultural Affiliation and Adjustment Among Male Mexican-American College Students," *Psychological Reports*, Vol. 55, 1984, pp. 855–860.

Gibson, M. A., "Accommodation Without Assimilation," paper presented at the Conference on Immigrant Students in California, University of California, San Diego, Center for U.S.-Mexican Studies, 1993.

Gibson, M. A., *Accommodation Without Assimilation: Sikh Immigrants in an American High School*, Ithaca, N.Y.: Cornell University Press, 1988.

Graham, M. A., "Acculturative Stress Among Polynesian, Asian, and American Students on the Brigham Young University-Hawaii Campus," *International Journal of Intercultural Relations*, Vol. 7, 1983, pp. 79–103.

Gray, M. J., E. Rolph, and Elan Melamid, *Immigration and Higher Education: Institutional Responses to Changing Demographics*, Santa Monica, Calif.: RAND, MR-751-AMF, 1996.

Greenwood, M. J., and J. M. McDowell, *The Labor Market Consequences of U.S. Immigration: A Survey*, Washington, D.C.: U.S. Department of Labor, Bureau of International Labor Affairs, 1990.

Grissmer, D. W., et al., *Student Achievement and the Changing American Family*, Santa Monica, Calif.: RAND, MR-488-LE, 1994.

Hanushek, E. A., "The Trade-Off Between Child Quantity and Quality," *Journal of Political Economy*, Vol. 100, 1992, pp. 84–117.

Hill, M. A., and J. O'Neill, "Family Endowment and the Achievement of Young Children with Special Reference to the Underclass," unpublished mimeo, 1993.

"Immigrant, U.S. Peers Differ Starkly in Schools," *Los Angeles Times*, February 22, 1996.

Kao, G., and M. Tienda, "Optimism and Achievement: The Educational Performance of Immigrant Youth," *Social Science Quarterly*, Vol. 76, No. 1, March 1995.

Klein, S. P., et al., *Interactions Among Gift-Aid Programs in Indiana*, Santa Monica, Calif.: RAND, R-4218-LE, 1992.

Kohn, M. L., and C. Schooler, *Work and Personality: An Inquiry into the Impact of Social Stratification*, Ablex Publishing Corporation, 1983.

Koretz, D., *Trends in the Postsecondary Enrollment of Minorities*, Santa Monica, Calif.: RAND, R-3948-FF, 1990.

Manski C. F., and D. A. Wise, *College Choice in America*, Cambridge, Mass.: Harvard University Press, 1983.

Meana, F. J., A. M. Padilla, and M. Maldonado, "Acculturative Stress and Specific Coping Strategies Among Immigrant and Later Generation College Students," *Hispanic Journal of Behavioral Sciences*, Vol. 9, 1987, pp. 207–225.

McDonnell, L. M., and P. T. Hill, *Newcomers in American Schools: Meeting the Educational Needs of Immigrant Youth*, Santa Monica, Calif.: RAND, MR-103-AWM/PRIP, 1993.

Ogbu, J. U., "Immigrant and Involuntary Minorities in Comparative Perspective," in Margaret A. Gibson and John U. Ogbu (eds.), *Minority Status and Schooling: A Comparative Study of Immigrant and Involuntary Minorities*, New York and London: Garland Publishing, Inc., 1991, pp. 3–33.

Ogle, L. T., and N. Alsalam (eds.), *The Condition of Education 1990: Volume 1, Elementary and Secondary Education*, National Center for Education Statistics, U.S. Department of Education, Washington, D.C.: Government Printing Office, 1990.

Padilla, A. M., M. Alvarez, and K. J. Lindholm, "Generational Status and Personality Factors as Predictors of Stress in Students," *Hispanic Journal of Behavioral Sciences*, Vol. 8, 1986, pp. 275–288.

Pruitt, F. J., "The Adaptation of African Students to American Society," *International Journal of Intercultural Relations*, Vol. 2, 1978, pp. 90–118.

Rumbaut, R. G., "The New Californians: Comparative Research on the Educational Progress of Immigrant Children," in R. G. Rumbaut and W. A. Cornelius (eds.), *California's Immigrant Children*, San Diego, Calif.: Center for Mexican Studies, University of California, 1995, pp. 17–70.

Rumbaut, R. G., *Immigrant Students in California Public Schools: A Summary of Current Knowledge*, report prepared for Johns Hopkins University, Baltimore, MD.: Center for Research on Effective Schooling for Disadvantaged Students, 1990.

Schoeni, R. F., K. F. McCarthy, and G. Vernez, *Pursuing the American Dream: Economic Progress of Immigrant Men in California and the Nation*, Santa Monica, Calif.: RAND, MR-763-IF/FF, 1996.

Searle, W., and C. Ward, "Prediction of Psychological and Sociocultural Adjustment During Cross-Cultural Transitions," *International Journal of Intercultural Relations*, 1990, pp. 449–464.

Suárez-Orozco, M. M., and C. E. Suárez-Orozco, "The Cultural Patterning of Achievement Motivation: A Comparison of Mexican, Mexican Immigrants, Mexican American, and Non-Latino White American Students," in R. G. Rumbaut and W. A. Cornelius (eds.), *California's Immigrant Children*, San Diego, Calif.: Center for Mexican Studies, University of California, 1995, pp. 161–190.

Suárez-Orozco, M. M., and C. E. Suárez-Orozco, "Hispanic Cultural Psychology: Implications for Education Theory and Research," paper presented at a workshop on immigrant children in California schools, Center for U.S.-Mexican Studies, University of California, San Diego, January 23, 1993.

Sue, S., and N. W. S. Zane, "Academic Achievement and Socioemotional Adjustment Among Chinese University Students," *Journal of Counseling Psychology*, Vol. 32, 1985, pp. 570–579.

Tracey, T. J., and W. E. Sedlacek, "The Relationship of Noncognitive Variables to Academic Success: A Longitudinal Comparison by Race," *Journal of College Student Personnel*, 1985, pp. 405–410.

U.S. Department of Education, *Digest of Education Statistics 1993*, National Center for Education Statistics, Washington, D.C.: U.S. Government Printing Office, 1993.

Wilson, R., and M. J. Justiz, "Minorities in Higher Education: Confronting a Time Bomb," *Educational Record*, Vol. 68, 1987–1988, pp. 9–14.